I0210369

ESSAYS ON COVID-19

Edited by

Niall MacGiolla Bhuí, PhD

and

Phil Noone, PhD

Essays on COVID-19

www.thedoccheck.com
www.dissertationdoctorsclinic.com
www.thedoccheck.com

Copyright © Individual Authors & TheDocCheck.Com (2022).
Each Author asserts the moral right to be identified as the author of their work.

ISBN: 978-1-7391012-2-0

Chapters Reviewed by Daragh Fleming and Karen Gallen.

Images sourced Niall MacGiolla Bhuí.

TheDocCheck.Com is committed to diversity, inclusion and equality.
We print all our books on forestry sustainable paper.

No part of this book can be reproduced without the written permission of the Publisher.
Please contact info@thedoccheck.com for information.

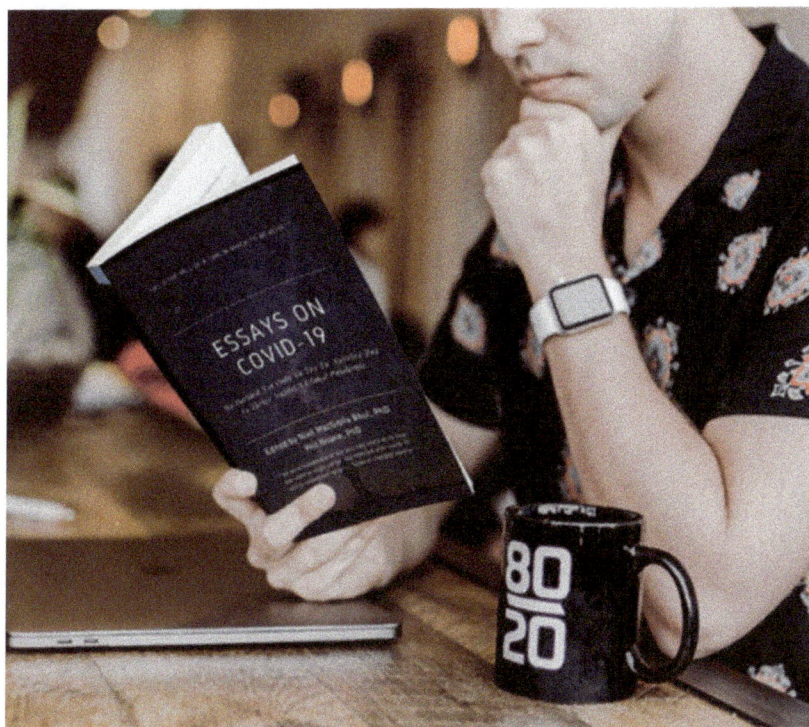

Covid-19 and the New World

The first case of the 2020 coronavirus disease COVID-19 was recorded in Italy on February 21 in Lombardy (Codogno). On April 15, 78 days later, COVID-19 had caused the death of 136,116 people around the world ([World Health Organization, 2021](#)).

Like so many people, I have a personal interest in the pandemic as my daughter was a pupil in a primary school in Craughwell, Galway at this time. Hers was the first class in Ireland to be requested by the government to isolate in their homes. We had a visit from the Health Services Executive ambulance service where the health worker was dressed from head to foot in Haz Mat gear. She came into our home and sprayed our hall. She then went upstairs to my daughter's room where she proceeded to test her for the virus. Naturally, my then twelve-year-old was terrified at this intrusion. The test did not go well and caused her discomfort and some bleeding as the health worker was in the early stages of gaining testing expertise. Little did we know then how used we would all become to home testing kits. Neither were we aware of the profound change coming into our lives.

Covid-19 has been referred to as a "black swan event." It, quite literally, turned all of our worlds upside down and exposed deep structural inequalities and social issues. Surely, historians will come to recount this period as viscerally destructive and they will wonder how did we cope and what have we learned? 'Perception' and 'response' will sum up this era. Have governments, agencies of the state and individuals demonstrated flexibility? Have we all successfully adapted to the many crisis challenges that unfolded week in, week out? Most importantly to the authors in this volume, has resiliency been demonstrated?

Interestingly, science had already taken a massive hit pre pandemic, not helped it seems fair to say, by the US Trump Administration. Science, then, during the pandemic became somewhat abnormal and reactive. It was ambiguous and this contributed to a pervasive sense of helplessness.

It seems to me, a key take away nugget for us all is that we, as individuals, must be much more critically reflexive in our thinking around our political systems than we have heretofore (**Bonanno** et al, 2010). The imbalance of political power demonstrated since the first awareness of the 'bat disease' has been truly shocking. Our various governments, legislative bodies, health systems and national and local authorities largely failed to communicate with us in a transparent manner – adding to a culture of mistrust and distrust.

Perhaps we have learned that what we took for granted, *certainty* may have surreptitiously morphed into *uncertainty*. And, perhaps, this will now be the new normal. Alongside this unwelcome traveller is another new guest, 'anxiety'. The kind of guest that sneaks down in the middle of the night and cleans out the refrigerator.

On a more positive note, many commentators are looking to advocacy around psychological flexibility where we continue to recognise opportunity (Cooke et al, 2020). Hence, this book. Thus, we have asked some of our colleagues to share their experiences of Covid-19, but from a perspective of (somehow) coping, (somehow) being resilient but, most of all, continuing to appreciate and love this one and only precious life.

—Dr Niall MacGiolla Bhuí

References

Bonanno, G. A., Brewin, C. R., Kaniasty, K., La Greca, A. M. (2010). Weighing the costs of disaster: Consequences, risks, and resilience in individuals, families, and communities. Psychological Science in the Public Interest, 11(1), 1–49. https://doi.org/10.1177/1529100610387086

Cooke, J. E., Eirich, R., Racine, N., Madigan, S. (2020). Prevalence of posttraumatic and general psychological stress during COVID-19: A rapid review and meta-analysis. Psychiatry Research, 292, Article 113347. https://doi.org/10.1016/j.psychres.2020.113347

World Health Organization . (2021). WHO Coronavirus Disease (COVID-19) Dashboard—deaths. https://covid19.who.int/Google Scholar

Without Rice even the Cleverest Cannot Cook

As I reflect on our experience of Covid 19, I am immediately drawn to the work of sociologist Ulrich Beck, titled *'Risk Society: Towards a New Modernity'* ([1986],1992). Written in 1986, it has an incredible capacity to tap into the underlying anxieties and insecurities of our modern age. Central to Beck's thinking about risk, is that instead of occurring in the natural world, risks today are caused by the unintended consequences of modernisation itself. He believed that what makes the management of these risks so difficult is that *'there is nowhere to hide'*! A theme that runs through so many of the chapters in this book. The real issue, in Beck's view, is the inadequacy of the global and national institutions to cope with these global crisis. He speaks of a culture of public distrust in expert systems, a growing disquiet with the scientific community and governments or institutional bodies. I think this was part of our collective experience during the Pandemic.

Our book *Essays on Covid 19*, is timely. It is of national and global importance to capture how ordinary citizens of Ireland lived, worked and coped with the frightening upheaval in their everyday lives. To rely solely on scientific laboratory text would be an omission. This book illuminates the human spirit, resilience, coping, a muddling through and survival.

To paraphrase a Chinese proverb:

'without rice, even the cleverest cannot cook'

—Dr. Phil Noone

Reference

Beck U. (1992) Risk Society: Towards a New Modernity. London: Sage.

Table of Contents

SEA TEMPERATURES AT BLACKROCK 2021.

DEGREES CELSIUS.

2021	JAN	FEB	MAR	APR	MAY	JUN	JUL	AUG	SEP	OCT	NOV	DEC
MIN	3.6	4.9	7.3	8.4	9.1	13.3	13.8	16.0				
MAX	8.9	9.1	11.3	11.6	15.8	16.3	22.0	19.4				

Coldest water readings.   25 Jan.

Warmest water readings.   22 Jul.   Evening reading 17 Jul of 23.2 degrees Celsius.

2020	JAN	FEB	MAR	APR	MAY	JUN	JUL	AUG	SEP	OCT	NOV	DEC
MIN	5.2	6.0	5.8	8.5	9.7	12.5	14.5	15.5	12.0	10.5	7.8	6.1
MAX	8.7	8.0	9.3	11.3	17.0	16.7	17.2	18.9	16.5	14.5	11.0	10.6

Coldest water readings.   19 Jan.

Warmest water readings.   12 Aug.

2019	JAN	FEB	MAR	APR	MAY	JUN	JUL	AUG	SEP	OCT	NOV	DEC
MIN	5.0	6.0	7.9	8.5	11.0	13.7	15.5	16.1	14.1	11.1	6.9	4.5
MAX	9.4	10.6	11.0	13.4	14.5	16.5	19.2	18.3	16.0	14.7	13.0	10.0

Coldest water readings.   17 Dec.

Warmest water readings.   29 July.

2018	JAN	FEB	MAR	APR	MAY	JUN	JUL	AUG	SEP	OCT	NOV	DEC
MIN	5.8	5.0	5.0	6.2	10.5	13.6	15.3	14.9	11.2	9.6	7.0	7.2
MAX	7.1	6.5	8.4	13.0	15.0	19.3	18.0	17.0	16.9	13.9	11.0	9.0

Coldest water readings.   16 Feb and 02 Mar.

Warmest water readings.   30 Jun.

Compiled by P.McNamara.

The Blue Antidote: Sea Swimming as a Resilience Mechanism to Covid-19

Niall MacGiolla Bhuí, PhD

One Hell of a Time to be Alive

> *"To those who do not know the world is on fire,*
> *I have nothing to say."*
>
> —Bertolt Brecht

The recent emergence of the Covid-19 pandemic has affected all aspects of daily life since it was first reported on the 31st of December 2019 by the Wuhan Municipal Health Commission in China (WHO, 2020). Following this, the virus spread rapidly across the globe with the Irish government reporting its first case on the 26th of February 2020 (HSE, 2021).

Niall MacGiolla Bhuí, PhD

This is one hell of a time in which to be alive. Truly. I should declare at the outset of this chapter that I've always been interested in the Jungian concept of the 'hero's journey', one where an 'ordinary' individual heeds a call to arms; to great adventure and ventures out into the world to face enormous struggles and suffering, but returns home (to a location and within *self*) with heightened self-awareness. And so we are living in and through a time of the ages where a seismic shift is occurring as I write this. Tensions – so, so many tensions have come to govern public 'speak' – over expertise, crisis, leadership, trust, and protection – and will loom even larger in coming months and, in all probability, years ahead. It seems reasonable to suggest that a 'politicisation of the pandemic' has throttled the life out of how we understood the democratic process to be in many countries. Ireland is no exception. Are we living in and through a pandemic or scamdemic? Oh, and May 2022 has brought us the gift of Monkeypox.

We are also witnessing, once again, and we have already seen this with the 'migrant crisis' across Europe over the past decade - that we are all connected. To disregard one country or one people is to, ultimately, disregard all of us. International, national, regional and local political decisions and, indeed, non-decisions have come back to haunt us all.

The Covid incarnation in 2021, Omicron, supposedly has its origins in poverty stricken India and moved to poverty stricken South Africa and then travelled to the West. It did not need to be so if we had managed and shared resources in a much more equitable manner. Notably, it is the poorest people in the poorest countries who have the highest mortality rates.

Are We Living in a Global Reset?

But, hidden away in all of this, there's an interesting question. Are we experiencing a global "financal reset" unbeknownst to ourselves? If so, why? And, if so, whom is controlling this? Are we part of a global trial of financial rather than the more obvious medical crisis? Is all this really about banking and digital currencies? These questions deserve to be asked.

The UCLA based sociologist, Rogers Brubakers (2017:np), writing about the situation in north America, notes that "the pandemic has not generated a coherent or large-scale populist response. But the lockdowns have created a reservoir of popular anger, and they have fostered the emergence of a populist mood among substantial parts of the population.

They have heightened distrust of expertise, exacerbated antipathy to intrusive government regulation, and amplified scepticism toward elite overprotectiveness". I believe he is correct in this.

A central difficulty in this absolute mess, and it is a mess by any measure, is what people seem to believe or 'know' about the pandemic (and I'm including gatekeepers and stakeholders in this) has been, to date, completely chaotic and ever-changing. The worrying consistent shift in public messaging from government and health officials, has resulted in an embedding of a sense of polarisation in communities.

The official media ecosystem seems only to allow one narrative, which I find deeply disturbing for a supposed democracy. There are daily vocal challenges to 'expertise' and no wonder – everyone is winging it in this new global epidemiological landscape. Literally everyone. This contra opinion is largely confined to social media so more and more people are moving to these sources for 'truth'.

So, What Can We Do? What Should We Do?

Dodge et al. (2012: 228) define wellbeing as "the balance point between an individual's resource pool and the challenges faced". How can we manage our own mental health? Well, I took to sea swimming with two very good friends.

We have a major *resource* in Galway; Blackrock Diving Tower in Salthill. It's an iconic landmark. This, we thought, might provide some balance in a world spinning out of control around us. A sense of balance is core to Csikszentmihalyi's (1975) concept of flow, which he understands to be a state of mind that occurs when a person is so deeply engaged in something that time seems to stop for them (Nakamura & Csikszentmihalyi, 2014). We really wanted and needed time to stop – at least for a while.

I have written elsewhere of how sea swimming causes time to stop for me (MacGiolla Bhuí, 2021). It is one of the only locations and times I can fully switch off from all the day to day stresses of work schedules and deadlines because I have to give all my concentration to not potentially drowning (a fear I've had since twelve years old when my older brother, Joe, had to save me when I dived into the water and found myself way out of my depth).

Open Water Sea Swimming

There has been a massive increase in interest in swimming in what are termed 'natural bodies of water' in Ireland (as opposed to swimming pools) and this has been noted across recent qualitative and quantitative research (Costello et al., 2019; Depledge & Bird, 2009; Foley, 2015; Gascon et al., 2017; MacGiolla Bhuí, 2021; Nutsford et al., 2016; Swain, 2019). However, there is still limited research exploring this phenomenon specific to Salthill in Galway.

The research that exists on sea swimming is clear that immersion in nature, more generally, and water in particular, contribute very substantively to our mental and physical health (Noone, 2021; van Tulleken et al., 2018). The active promotion of 'blue space' for wellness and wellbeing will gather very significant momentum over coming years, I am certain.[1]

---

[1] There are several research initiatives and programmes: 'Sea, Ocean and Public Health in Europe' (SOPHIE), the UK Blue Gyms and the Irish programme, 'Nature and

Niall MacGiolla Bhuí, PhD

Several times a week throughout 2021 and into May 2022 at the time of completing this chapter, we headed out into the cold waters of the Atlantic despite the rain, hail, cold and intemperate weather that is the norm for us here in Galway. We started with a couple of minutes immersion in the basin of Blackrock as we found the water temperature so cold and, gradually, over a period of months we were able to stay in the water longer and longer, eventually swimming out and back to those magical orange safety buoys. And out. And back again. I smiled reading the projected temperature for today, May 25th 2022 as we have swam amidst hailstones falling on us in just 5 degree waters...

"Today water temperature in Galway is 12.7degrees. In general, this water temperature is unacceptable for swimming. But hardened people can afford to in such water for 5-10 minutes. In any case, the general weather is also important. So, the air temperature at the same time will reach 12degrees." (SeaTemperature.Net)

It's now August 2022, so we have completed seventeen months of sea swimming together. Early on, we established a routine, which is very important. Psychology notes the importance of positive habit formation and Noone (2020) argues that 'with time and repeated

---

Environment to Attain and Restore Health' ('NEAR Health') which seek to engage multidisciplinary research to understand the health benefits associated with water engagement and to inform and involve policymakers and practitioners to promote health to the broader population.

performance of the activity, triggered by contextual cues, the importance of goals lesson as time goes on'. We would park up our cars and then walk 7kilometres before our swim. We had, at least to an extent, warmed up inside prior to swimming – even though our clothes were often wet through. I managed about a week in my wetsuit before my two friends, Phil and Cliona, encouraged me out of it. They were swimming without wearing one so why shouldn't I? I ditched it in January 2021, and my wetsuit now lies lonesome in a wet bag in the Clinic office.

Of course, open water cold swimming is about much more than the obvious physical challenge of ridding oneself of one's clothes and stepping out into the water from the metal ladders. It is a mental challenge.[2]

We decided that there were so many other mental challenges around us that we had absolutely no control over, that we would initiate one that we *did* have control over. We would brave the elements and brave the water and we *chose* to go for it. At the start there were so few people around us that Blackrock in Salthill felt like our own little fiefdom. But, over the months, we noticed more and more hardy souls also deciding to take ownership of stress reduction and healthy endeavour for themselves, on their own

---

[2] It's important to note the potential dangers with evidence across several scientific studies of a reduction in cerebral artery blood flow, which at very cold water temperatures can cause syncope [fainting] characterized by drowsiness, blurred vision, and a loss of responsiveness in some individuals.

terms. As an aside, none of the three of us contacted colds or flus over the past fifteen months and, thankfully, none of us contracted Covid at the time of completing this chapter. We are our own phenomenological study.

Ultimately, open water sea swimming was a multi-faceted experience imbued with deep and long-lasting meaning for each of us. We have found it to be a necessary venture for maintaining and, crucially, enhancing our mental and emotional wellbeing. We were inundated over the past two years as to how one might or might not become infected with Covid-19 and its subsequent variants. Science changed weekly. But, in the cold water we felt and feel safe. In the Atlantic waters we feel impervious to the global pandemic. Here, only being in the moment truly matters.

References

Brubaker R (2017) Why populism? Theory and Society 46(5): 357–385. DOI:10.1007/s11186-017-9301-7.

Brubaker, R. Paradoxes of Populism During the Pandemic. [online] Thesis Eleven Project on Living and Thinking Crisis. 2020. URL: https://thesiseleven.com/2020/07/13/paradoxes-of-populism-during-the-pandemic/ Accessed 28th August 2022.

Canovan M (1999) Trust the People! Populism and the Two Faces of Democracy. Political Studies 47(1): 2–16. DOI: 10.1111/1467-9248.00184.

Costello, L., McDermott, M.L., Patel, P. & Dare, J. (2019) 'A lot better than medicine', Self- organised ocean swimming groups as facilitators for healthy ageing', Health & place, 60(1), pp.102212.

Covey S. R. (2020) The 7 Habits of Highly Effective People. New York: Simon & Schuster.

Csikszentmihalyi M, (1975) Beyond Boredom and Anxiety. San Francisco: Jossey-Bass.

Csikszentmihalyi M. (2002) Flow: The Classic Work on How to Achieve Happiness. London: Rider Books.

Depledge, M.H. & Bird, W.J. (2009) 'The Blue Gym: health and wellbeing from our coasts', Marine Pollution Bulletin, 58(7), p.947-948.

Dodge R. & Daly A. & Huyton J. & Sanders L. (2012) The challenge of defining well-being. International Journal of Wellbeing. 2(3), 222-235.

Eyal, G (2019) The Crisis of Expertise. Cambridge, UK; Medford, MA: Polity Press.

Niall MacGiolla Bhuí, PhD

Foley, R. (2015) 'Swimming in Ireland: Immersions in therapeutic blue space', *Health & Place, 35*, pp.218-225.

Gascon, M., Zijlema, W., Vert, C., White, M.P. & Nieuwenhuijsen, M.J. (2017) 'Outdoor blue spaces, human health and well-being: a systematic review of quantitative studies', *International journal of hygiene and environmental health, 220*(8), pp.1207- 1221.

MacGiolla Bhuí, N. (2021) Escaping from a diagnosis of disconnection, in Mental Health For Millennials Vol 5 On Resiliency. Pp1-8. Galway. Book Hub Publishing.

Noone, P. (2020). Habit formation and its impact on wellbeing, in Mental Health For Millennials Vol 4 On Wellbeing. pp. Galway. Book Hub Publishing.

Noone, P. (2021) *Blue space connectedness and building resilience*, in Mental Health For Millennials Vol 5 On Resiliency. pp9-22. Galway. Book Hub Publishing.

Nutsford, D., Pearson, A.L., Kingham, S. & Reitsma, F. (2016) 'Residential exposure to visible blue space (but not green space) associated with lower psychological distress in a capital city', *Health & place, 39*(1), pp.70-78.

Swain, K. (2019) 'The metamorphoses of wild swimming', The lancet. Psychiatry, 6(10), pp.

814-815.

van Tulleken, C., Tipton, M., Massey, H. & Harper, C.M. (2018) 'Open water swimming as a treatment for major depressive disorder', BMJ Case Reports, pp. 1-3.

URLs

https://seatemperature.net/current/ireland/galway-sea-temperature

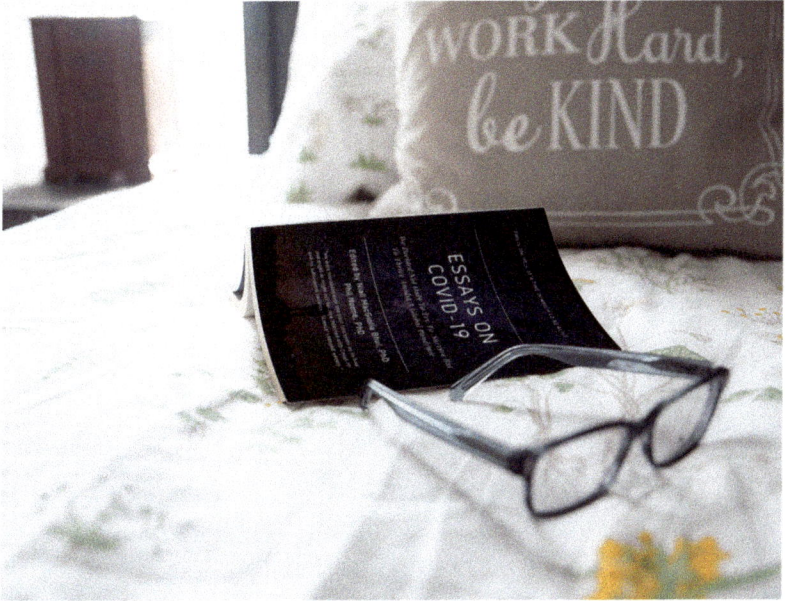

Uncertainty and Fear in a Time of Pandemic 'Creating Bubbles in the Sea Scape'!

Phil Noone, PhD

Introduction

Fear is contagious. Like the Covid-19 virus, it spreads fast and furious amongst individuals, peoples, and populations. We are interconnected, relational beings. It is an undeniable human desire to connect with one another, to share fun moments and to embed ourselves in the social fabric of our society.

Yet, the pandemic, the Covid-19 virus, the onset of restrictions, lockdowns resulted in our disconnect. Our normal, social conversational spaces were forced to close, our sense of connectedness, our belongingness toppled by the shattered, scattered, splintered impact of the pandemic.

Societal divisions that lay dormant pre-pandemic multiplied into furious debates, 'vaxed versus non-vaxed', 'jabbed versus non-jabbed'. Even the language used fuelled and amplified the diversity of opinion that existed. This sometimes toxic use of language heightened our collective and individual sense of fear, confusion and uncertainty. The power of the politic versus the left wing anti-establishment, activists who lobbied fiercely against the vaccination programme, the need for Covid certificates, the wearing of masks, social distancing and other restrictive measures introduced by governments and their advisors to try and control the virus spread.

This diversity of opinion instead of creating a sensible and knowledgeable, balanced debate generated a fear and uncertainty about doing the 'right thing', making the 'right choices' for the protection of ourselves, our families and society.

The Four Horsemen of Fear

Schimmentic et al (2020) in Clinical Neuropsychiatry write about the 'Four Horsemen of Fear', an integrated model of understanding fear experienced during the Covid-19 pandemic. This model consists of 4 interrelated domains that operate on a psychological level to include the bodily, interpersonal, cognitive and behavioural features of fear:

ESSAYS ON COVID-19

1. Fear of the body/fear for the body
2. Fear of significant others/fear for significant others
3. Fear of not knowing/fear of knowing
4. Fear of taking action/fear of inaction.

The 'Four Horsemen of Fear' (the four domains of fear) during the Covid-19 pandemic is made up of two seemingly opposite aspects of each domain. It proposes a dialectical structure of identified fears where each element of fear may co-exist with its apparent opposite. Thus, fear in this model is not organised in a hierarchical manner but instead suggests an ever changing dynamic where different elements operate in a complexity that shifts and alters the fear experience.

As a Mindfulness Teacher, I found this model fascinating and very realistic. The body is the first organiser of human experience (Stern 1985) yet it is so often denied or hidden by a preoccupation of our sense of 'doing' and 'busy-iness' in our everyday. Van der Kolk (2014) in her book 'The Body Keeps the Score', explains how the body experiences events that pose harm to our physical and psychological well-being. In Mindfulness we speak of the 'heart-mind-body' interconnectedness, each impacting and being impacted by one other (Kabat-Zinn 2013).

During Covid-19, physical vulnerability existed because the body represented the potential source through which the virus spread and entered the body, a 'body betrayal' via infection and possible death (Schimmentic et al 2020:42). In addition, there was an increased need to protect and care for the body. In this sense, the body was not viewed as a threat but as a treasure that might be lost and therefore needed to be protected.

Aristotle said in Politics (Lord, 2003) that human beings are by their nature 'social animals'. Because interpersonal relationships form our attachments and give us a sense of belonging and security (Bowlby 1988), recommendations of 'social distancing' created a fear that getting too close to even those in our family circle posed a threat to our safety.

The fear of 'knowing and not knowing' related to the cognitive aspect of the virus, knowledge of which was ever shifting and changing. The daily news feeds on mass media and social media reporting on the numbers of patients infected or dead added to the fear experienced and was often overwhelming. In addition, the frantic searching for Covid-19 related information online, for some, exacerbated fear, often leading to heightened state of anxiety and distress. And on the other side, fear of not knowing resulted in loss of control, also exacerbating the fear experience.

Much of our lives are made up of habit formation (Noone 2018), intentional planning and action. These are not always reflexive but are planned and subjectively meaningful (Davidson 1980). As indicated in the first three domains, fears in our body, at the interpersonal and cognitive level impact on our behaviour. For example, fear of visiting parents and need to protect them may conflict with the desire to help and reduce their isolation. Thus, both action and inaction can result in increased fear.

Creating Insular Bubbles of Inclusion and Exclusion

During this time, we were instructed to live in what I describe as an 'artificial bubble'. Cocoon was the terms officialdom given to it, to remain at home, restrict movement and generally avoid unnecessary contact or as Teresa Mannion in a windswept news report in 2015, cautioned the nation 'to avoid unnecessary journeys'. I believe the pandemic created insular 'bubbles' of inclusion and exclusion by generating fear and uncertainty. Exclusion of some, particularly older people, who living alone, opened their windows to say hello, fearful of opening their doors in case the virus swamped them. In nursing homes, our television screens showed scenes of older people waving from upstairs windows to loved ones below who came to visit. Hundreds denied the right to say a proper goodbye to loved ones who had died from the ravages of the virus as it attacked our physical bodies and invaded the social fabric of our lives.

Two years later and our sense of fear is heightened when we are close by someone in a supermarket and we notice they are not wearing a mask! Our initial tentative steps down the adaptability route are now cemented into a conditioning of right and wrong.

Perhaps, in a broader sense it represents our need to fit in, to be like everyone else, to not be different, singled out. What have we become in two short years? It frightens me in a sense to observe and be part of blind obedience! But it also taught me that our adaptability is immense.

The Bubble of Swim Pod 3

Swim Pod 3 came into existence during the pandemic when three of us decided to sea swim every day in the cold Atlantic waters off Blackrock Diving Tower in Galway. Its impact was incredible!

It created certainty. In uncertain times. It offered routine. When our normal life routine was interrupted. It bonded friendship and cemented our commitment to our daily dose of vitamin sea! The sea is always changing, never the same, uncertain in temperament. And yet, it created a certainty, a stability in our lives. It gave a unique sense of being present, of being in the 'now' as we swam in temperatures of 7 degrees and lower. That raw sensation of 'now' as we gasped from the cold flooding our bodies with that first jump in! The inclusiveness of the community of swimmers at Blackrock, Galway, Ireland as we hurriedly changed post swim, our topic of conversation never the pandemic but instead, the water temperatures of the day!

Heading home. Warm fire. Chat. Family. Simple pleasures. The certainty of the key opening in the front door. And thus, the pandemic brought me closer, bonded me stronger, connected me to my home and the people in it. I created and recreated, strengthened and restrengthened, cherished certainties in my every day.

Sea swimming created a new and treasured bubble of connectedness for me and my Swim Pod. I share one such evening with you. The sea was so calm, a dark blue, reflecting the deep blue sky above. Golden reds and greens were tinting the sky amidst the low-lying scattering of clouds. No wind. The sea inviting. Dusk. Fading light. Aha, the moon appeared. And I swam. Sun sinking behind. Moon shimmering above. Magical beauty. The water dancing with the rays of setting sun. I swam some more. One stroke effortlessly following the other. Gently dipping, rippling the water. Conscious it was very cold. We wanted to swim further. Longer. But decided to turn back towards our safety net of the Blackrock Diving Tower. Water temperature a mere 7.2 degrees! Hands numb. Feet numb. We emerged. Stiff with cold. Calm. Elated. Happy.

I stood and watched the ocean. Listened. The lap of the waves. And realised my angst of the day, my fear had totally disappeared. My sense of freedom returned. My constricting thoughts vanished. Snapped. Carried out to sea like driftwood. Gone. No longer firing the familiar neural circuit of uncertainty. Certainty enveloped me. Calmness surrounded me. I felt confident. Untroubled. I was in the power of 'now', knowing that the next day would bring a new opportunity to sea swim, to embrace the elements as a means of enhancing my own emotional resilience in these uncertain times. The pandemic will pass, but the emotional resilience, connectedness and power of the ocean and Mindfulness will remain in their ever-expansive space of 'Ocean Mindfulness'.

To link this experience to the 4 Horsemen of Fear:

1.   Fear of the body/fear for the body:

Research on cold water swimming tells us that our immune system is activated and strengthened when we swim (MacGiolla Bhui 2021). We looked for control over our bodies in the water, embraced it and were embraced by the ever lapping of the waves. Our bodies and the water existed in tandem with each other, resulting in a deeply immersive experience.

2.   Fear of significant others/fear for significant others

There was no fear of significant others, we swam as one, we connected with each other in our own sea bubble. We met and enjoyed the banter and chat that was an intrinsic part of the inclusiveness of the swimming community at Blackrock Diving Tower in Galway.

3. Fear of not knowing/fear of knowing

During our sea swimming, nothing mattered apart from the sea, the coldness of the water, our bodies as we swan, the beauty of the surrounding sea scape. The fear of knowing or not knowing did not exist because we only lived in the moment of 'now' in the present-ness of awareness that was the sea swim. For that short time each day, Covid-19 and the pandemic floated out of existence.

4. Fear of taking action/fear of inaction.

We took action to enhance our own mental well-being, we incorporated sea swimming into our daily lives so that it became embedded in our habit-formation and we adapted by taking control over our bodies, heart and minds and enjoying it.

Conclusion

Dealing with the uncertainty and fear of the pandemic meant for me, creating a bubble, finding a certainty in the power and purpose of 'Ocean Mindfulness' and sea swimming, as each stroke follows another and as each gentle wave dampens the sand to reveal its hidden wonders.

References

Bowlby J. (1988) A Secure Base: Clinical Applications of Attachment Theory. London: Routledge.

Davidson D. (1980) *Essay on Actions and Events.* Oxford, UK: Oxford University Press.

Kabat-Zinn (2013) Full Catastrophe Living: How to Cope with Stress, Pain and Illness using Mindfulness Meditation. London: Piatus.

Lord S. (2003) *Aristotle's Politics.* Chicago: University of Chicago Press.

MacGiolla Bhui (2021) Escaping from a Diagnosis of Disconnection: Our Pod of three Take to the Sea Embracing the Wild Atlantic Way and Resiliency. In: *Mental Health for Millennials* Vol 5, MacGiolla Bhui N. & Noone P (eds) Galway, Ireland: Book Hub Publishing.

Noone P (2020) Habit Formation and its Impact on Well-being. In: *Mental Health for Millennials* Vol 4, MacGiolla Bhui N. & Noone P (eds) Galway, Ireland: Book Hub Publishing.

Schimmenti A. & Billieux J. & Starcevic V. (2020) The Four Horsemen of Fear: An Integrated Model of Understanding Fear Experiences during the Covid-19 Pandemic. *Clinical Neuropsychiatry.* 17(2). 41-45.

Stern D.N. (1985) The Interpersonal World of the infant: A view from Psychoanalysis and Development Psychology. New York: Basic Books.

Van der Kolk (2014) The Body Keeps the Score: Mind, Brian and Body in the Transformation of Trauma. Great Britain: Penguin.

Allowing Myself to Thrive During Covid-19

Dr. Mary Helen Hensley

Introduction

I consider myself truly fortunate when it comes to Covid…not because I had it and survived it, but because of the state I was in physically, emotionally and spiritually when we danced. As a chiropractor, metaphysical healer, and student of the human experience, I have invested a lifetime in one simple concept which allowed me thrive, not just survive, the Covid experience.

The human body is designed to serve the purpose of the soul.

When sensationalized information about this 'sinister new disease' began to headline every newsfeed at the beginning of March 2020, a tidal wave of fear washed over the global community, fuelled by terrifying images, statistics and predictions of unprecedented death tolls. No one was safe, everyone was at risk, and the world began to retract in fear. I made a phone call to one of my closest friends and asked two things.

"Can I come visit?" to which she immediately replied, "Of course." My second question was one which most people thought unfathomable, ridiculous, selfish, even.

"I intend to pick up Covid on the way. I want to *know it* from the inside out, study it and help alleviate the fear and misconceptions around it…are you okay with that?"

"Let's do it!" she said, without a moment of hesitation.

Hopping on a Jet Plane

Long story short, that's exactly what I did. I jumped on a plane to L.A. on March 12th, and by March 13th, I began to show the first symptoms. A wicked sore throat, pounding headache and high temperature preceded a sudden loss of taste and smell, (which would take nearly three months to return). My friend, Angelica, began testing me daily, with an elaborate, frequency-based bio-resonance system. Initially, we marvelled at the rapid depletion of things like zinc and magnesium in my body, but we quickly began to see a very curious pattern emerge. As things such as Aspergillosis (black mould), heavy metal toxicity, and radiation poisoning began to surface, we observed that my body appeared to be using Covid to 'time travel'. Frequency signatures began to appear of the Fifth Disease (a cousin of the Measles that I had in the third grade), Mononucleosis, or Glandular Fever, that I got after kissing my infected boyfriend when I was a junior in high school, and the subsequent Epstein-Barr, which plagued my late teens with chronic fatigue. Oh, there was that breast-cancer footprint from when I was twenty-two and wait... are you kidding me? Is that the Coxsackie Virus I picked up from an insect bite while riding a camel in Africa? The list went on and on, as every strange ailment I had ever encountered began to show up and wave.

At this stage, my upper torso had erupted in hideous blisters we lovingly called 'the Bat pox', due to the flavour of the day on the news, which attempted to pin the source of CV-19 on some poor, unsuspecting Chinese bats. Each morning, I would crawl out of bed, jump on Facebook Live, and report to whoever cared to listen. I would share my symptoms, then go in to detail about what was showing up on my body scans. A few people unfollowed me, some were infuriated by my *cavalier* approach to the 'unknown', but the vast majority listened intently, asked questions and later told me that this daily report from the front-lines actually got them through the worst of times.

Doctor Heal Thyself

I'm a doctor, a facilitator of healing, and most importantly in these personal experiments, someone who doesn't fear death. This made me the perfect candidate to contract, dissect and report my findings. People's opinions about how I chose to dance with Covid simply didn't get a look in. Unconventional, to say the least, but that's me, in a pandemic and in every-day life. You see, that core belief that the body is designed to serve the soul's purpose, isn't just a catchy, new-age sentiment in my version of reality... I actually practice this principle, every single day of my life. Fears, doubts and uncertainty get a voice in my personal story; it would be preposterous to say they didn't. What they don't get, however, is a vote. By trusting the journey, by living every moment with the firm conviction that I will live until my soul's purpose is fulfilled, and I'll leave when I'm done, means that there really is no such thing as *crisis* in my life. I recognise, all too well, that there are many people who don't subscribe to this way of thinking. Folks like me tend to irritate those who live in a state of fight or flight, those who are easily swept up in panic, those who will join a cause without first doing the homework, or those who are genuinely just afraid. I accept that and I wouldn't dream of attempting to change the way they have come in to this world to experience their own unique version of life.

ESSAYS ON COVID-19

When I returned home to Ireland, nearly five months after 'the big dance', I jumped straight in to the most difficult and rewarding time in my twenty-five years as a doctor. And no, I wasn't ill for five months…it will probably come as no surprise that Angelica and I, along with my two daughters, thought that it would be a once-in-a lifetime experience to drive the whole way across America in the throes of a global pandemic. We set out on the iconic Route 66, dipped in to the deep south, before finally heading up to my mother's home in Virginia. We got to see what was happening out in the real world, not the fear-based bombardment from TV, radio and social media. We talked to real people and got excellent rates in some very empty hotels. We howled at a rising full moon from the top of Cathedral Rock (with a bunch of half-naked hippies and tarantulas) in Sedona, Arizona, forged the north and south rims of the glorious Grand Canyon, sweltered in the heat at Meteor Crater Natural Landmark, stood on a corner in Winslow, Arizona, roller-skated through Roswell, New Mexico wearing tin-foil hats, ate the world's largest steak in Texas, sipped whiskey with the great-grandson of an Irish immigrant in New Orleans, walked in the footsteps of Martin Luther King Jr. in Montgomery, Alabama, danced in *Hot*lanta, Georgia by moonlight, ate the best southern-fried chicken in South Carolina, climbed the peaks of the cool mountain forests of the Appalachians of North Carolina, and swam the lakes and frolicked at the foothills of the Blue Ridge Mountains in Virginia.

Dr. Mary Helen Hensley

Showing up to the Dance

My business never closed once I returned in September, 2020. In fact, I don't recall ever having been as busy as I've been these last two years. Maybe it was because so many things were closed; I'd like to believe that people began to rethink the importance of *how one shows up to the dance.* Suddenly, nearly overnight, suggestions I had been making for nearly a quarter of a century about tending to the health and well-being of the physical *and* emotional bodies *before* crisis set in...were finally starting to sink in.

To show up every day, stand firm in my own choices as to how I wanted to personally experience Covid, to guide, not judge...that is how I got through it. I couldn't imagine using the word 'cope' in my description of the last two years. I am an educator and a communicator, so I relied heavily on these two constants in my life to practice compassion and empathy. Humour has also been key, especially in those brief but very real moments where I felt like I might drown in other people's fear. I started making videos, coming up with fun (and funny) ways to present new perspectives, alternate possibilities, and friendly reminders that we were all having very different, unique and personal experiences with Covid; no one more real or more valid than the other. With talk of the Monkey Pox afoot, I've ordered a chimpanzee onesie and a banana handbag...*just in case.*

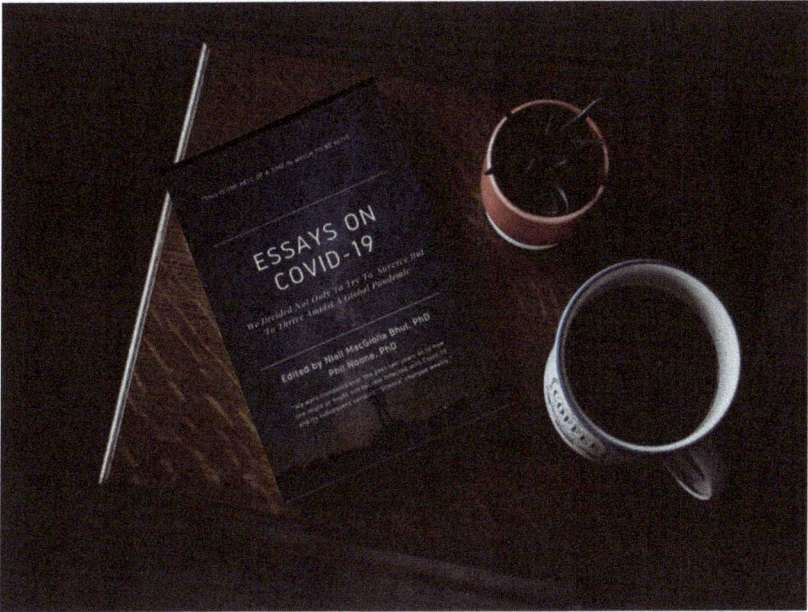

Cooking Through The Lens of Covid-19

Cathy Fitzgibbon aka The Culinary Celt

"Food can bring people together in a way nothing else could"
—Yotam Ottolenghi

Cooking Covid Style

The continuing COVID-19 pandemic, with its repetitive lockdown restrictions has greatly influenced our cooking rituals and eating patterns. Since the first lockdown restrictions were put in place in Ireland on the 12th of March 2020, research findings conducted from an online survey of 651 Irish food consumers by Henchion *et al.,* (2021) discovered what they refer to as a 'teachable moment', with more time spent at home preparing and consuming food for meals that in alternative circumstances would have taken place in different settings. Hammons and Robart (2021) support the view that, in times of uncertainty, routines such as mealtimes can help families maintain a sense of normality. It is the centrality of food that makes it a perfect vehicle to help provide security Fox (2003) and that has really shone through during the ongoing pandemic era, that we are all adapting to and seeking to find some semblance of sanity in!

Recent studies by Jansen *et al.,* (2021) show higher levels of stress amongst families during COVID-19 compared to the pre pandemic era. However, on a more positive note the shift in our worldwide eating behaviours has had a huge knock-on effect in terms of increased consumption of fresh foods at home (Adams *et al.,* 2020). This research is critically important in keeping with The Global Wellness Institute definition of wellness being "the active pursuit of activities, choices and lifestyles that lead to a state of holistic health" found at (www.globalwellnessinstitute.org) because it potentially informs family wellness efforts as we transition and learn to live alongside the virus in what we now label 'the new normal'.

Fuelling our Wellbeing

It is fair to say that during 'normal' daily life, time was not prioritised by many to prepare home-cooked meals. However with longer periods of time spent at home due to restrictions on our movements Covid-19 brought with it the opportunity to make wholesome meals, that in all honesty, were not previously prioritised by many in terms of time to cook.

According to the World Health Organisation found at (www.euro.who.int) good nutrition is crucial for health, particularly in times when our immune system may need to fight back. With this in mind, from the outset, when COVID-19 reached the shores here in Ireland I set about developing effective new food consumption rituals that would help keep me safe and protected from the potential effects of the virus.

Being a long-time advocate that eating the right foods and how boosting the intake of certain nutrients can greatly help increase overall energy reserves, thereby equipping us to cope better with life's challenges Fitzgibbon (2020) it became of paramount importance to have control, albeit in varying levels, over what I choose to cook and consume. With this in mind during my multitude of lockdown experiences, considerable emphasis was placed on the importance of healthy eating, physical fitness and my personal mental wellbeing.

Then there was one...

From the outset my lockdown experiences started with having to mindfully retrain my eating behaviour. To this effect and to make mealtimes work there was a need to embrace flying solo on this one! Being used to social settings for a large portion of pre-pandemic mealtimes it was completely new and unknown territory for me. Food is almost always shared (Fitzgibbon, 2019) so the start point was to find optimum ways to make solo food consumption rituals work.

It started with meal preparation in order to avoid food waste, as early on I was able to establish why I had embraced a lifestyle of frequently dining out with family and friends. A general practical observation (pardon the pun) is the fact that a large portion of the food we tend to have access to in local food stores, by and large, tends to lend itself to families and bigger household units. The next step was taking to social media to get inspiration and find ways that would work for me in my 'new normal' solo, working from home eating lifestyle. Wanting to be creative and adventurous, I found new cooking techniques from a variety of online platforms such as YouTube and Instagram which aided the restricted situation that I found myself needing to embrace. It was heart-warming to see chefs and restaurants find ways to pivot their businesses, by providing online recipe content and tutorials via their social media platforms, to support our new present-day way of living with Covid restrictions. This route proved fruitful as I learnt new ways to support the restaurant industry and enjoy this shared social connection, whilst eating alone, away from friends and family. Mealtimes would be different and I became more comfortable in the knowledge that this was the anchor point for exciting new culinary beginnings.

Room to Grow

Learning about myself and my body needs was the next challenge. I wanted to enjoy a varied diet similar to pre-Covid times. This was going to be interesting! My local farmers' market was closed for the first few lockdown periods so I had to turn to new innovative local online food community platforms as a source of stocking up on essential food items. The next project was to grow some of my own food, that initially consisted of a selection of herbs and tomatoes. These afforded me a huge sense of achievement and further appreciation for all the local work that producers put into providing us with a daily selection of their finest food offerings. With less commuting time, I was able to slow down and spend time outdoors connecting with nature. I was thankful to have more time to explore my local area and re-ignite my childhood memories of food foraging. Delicious berries were picked, eaten, and enjoyed, and I was also able to focus on my solo mindful eating techniques to enable further engagement of all of my senses. According to

Kabat-Zinn (1991:1-4), mindfulness is "paying attention in a particular way, on purpose, in the present moment, and nonjudgmentally". As an extension of this definition, mindful eating for me is about forming a good relationship with food, questioning who grew it, where it comes from and how it ended up on our plates. Covid, with its restrictions, provided me with the opportunity to further develop my daily rituals in this space.

The Future is Bright!

Covid has challenged us all in a variety of ways. There is now an apparent great shift and movement towards 'self-protection' and embracing more sustainable ways when it comes to food. According to Google Trends data, internet searches for 'food' and 'immune system' rose 670% globally in the first two weeks of March 2020 (www.kerry.com). We are now embracing this exciting era of creating a new relationship with cooking. Reported figures of over 50% of European consumers are now cooking more at home and attempting to cook a variety of original cuisines and recipes (www.kerry.com) and this makes it evident that Covid has completely changed how we view food in terms of its source, preparation and social context. Now let's also hope that we can sustain these newfound ways into the future, for the greater good of generations to come.

References

Adams E.L., Caccavale L.J., Smith D. and Bean M.K. (2020) "Food Insecurity, the Home Food Environment, and Parent Feeding Practices in the Era of COVID-19", *Obesity (Silver Spring)*, available at https://pubmed.ncbi.nlm.nih.gov/32762129/, accessed at 22:20, 1st December.

Fitzgibbon, C. (2020) *Mental Health For Millennials*, (Vol 4), Galway: Book Hub Publishing.

Fitzgibbon, C. (2019) *Mental Health For Millennials*, (Vol 3)", Galway: Book Hub Publishing.

Fox. R. (2003) "Food and Eating: An Anthropological Perspective", *Social Issues Research Centre*, available at http://www.sirc.org/publik/foxfood.pdf, accessed at 13:30, 2nd December.

Furlong, C. (2020) "5 Food and Beverage Trends in Europe During COVID-19", *KerryDigest Blog*, available at https://www.kerry.com/Insights/KerryDigest/2020/5-Food-and-Beverage-Trends-in-Europe-During-COVID-19, accessed at 20:04, 1st December.

Global Wellness Institute (n.d.) "What Is Wellness?", available at https://globalwellnessinstitute.org/what-is-wellness/, accessed at 09:25, 5th December.

Hammons, A. J. and Robart, R. (2021) "Family Food Environment during the COVID-19 Pandemic: A Qualitative Study", *Children*, Vol. 8 (5), p.354, available at https://www.mdpi.com/2227-9067/8/5/354, accessed at 12:52, 2nd December.

Henchion. M., McCarthy, S.N. and McCarthy, M. (2021) "A time of transition: changes in Irish food behaviour and potential implications due to the COVID-19 pandemic", *Irish Journal of Agricultural and Food Research*, available at https://www.scienceopen.com/hosted-document?doi=10.15212/ijafr-2020-0131, accessed at 21:05, 4th December.

Jansen E., Thapaliya G., Aghababian A., Sadler J., Smith K. and Carnell S. (2021) "Parental stress, food parenting practices and child snack intake during the COVID-19 pandemic", *Appetite*, available at https://pubmed.ncbi.nlm.nih.gov/33450298/, accessed at 16:20, 2nd December.

Kabat-Zinn J. (1991) Full Catastrophe Living. New York, N.Y: Dell Publishing, available at http://care1.htsun.ds.lib.uw.edu/wp-content/uploads/2020/05/mbsr_standards_of_practice_2014.pdf, accessed at 23:14, 1st December. Pp. 1-4.

World Health Organisation Regional Office for Europe (n.d.) *"Food and Nutrition Tips During Self-Quarantine"*, available at https://www.euro.who.int/en/health-topics/health-emergencies/coronavirus-covid-19/publications-and-technical-guidance/food-and-nutrition-tips-during-self-quarantine, accessed at 17:05, 2nd December.

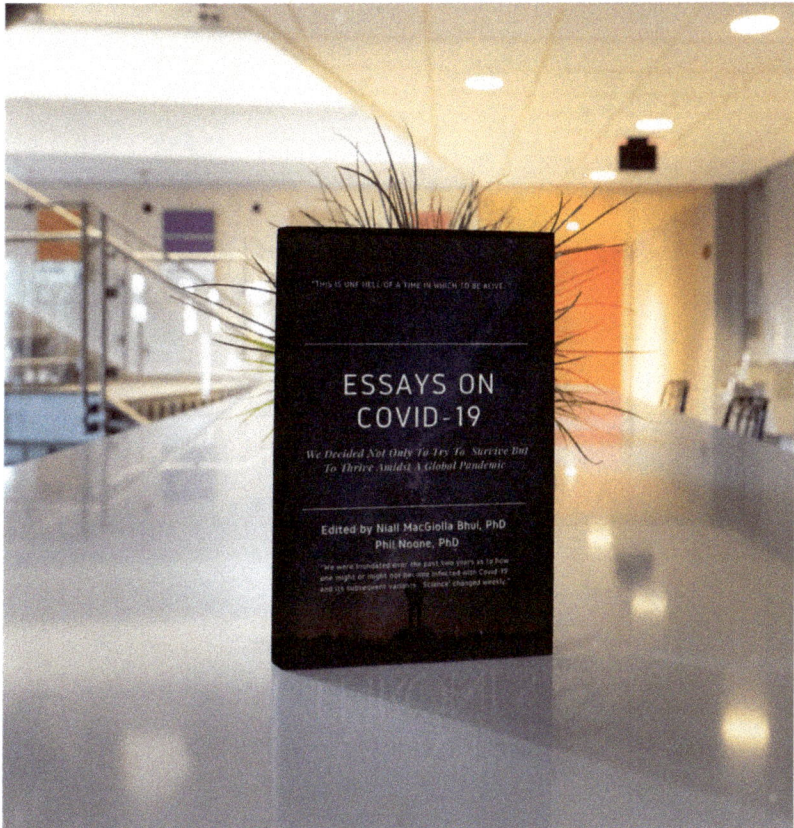

"THIS IS ONE HELL OF A TIME IN WHICH TO BE ALIVE."

ESSAYS ON COVID-19

*We Decided Not Only To Try To Survive But
To Thrive Amidst A Global Pandemic*

Edited by Niall MacGiolla Bhuí, PhD
Phil Noone, PhD

"We were inundated over the past two years as to how
one might or might not be one infected with Covid-19
and its subsequent variants. 'Science' changed weekly."

Imagining Sisyphus Happy

Daragh Fleming

Introduction

I remember the day we were sent home from work indefinitely, and subsequently permanently.

I still worked in an office back then. There was a sense of novelty, surrealness about it. None of it felt real, and those first three weeks to 'flatten the curve' were more exciting than anything else. The fear mixed with the uncertainty mustered up a unique sort of energy. You couldn't say it was boring.

Three weeks dissolved into months and then into two years. After a few months, it was clear to all of us that this virus wasn't going anywhere. We had to learn to live in new ways. Life stripped back, we had to cling onto those things we couldn't live without and accept a (hopefully) temporary loss of the more disposable parts of our existence. However, it is often these dispensable aspects which bring us a sense of happiness, comfort and meaning. And so we had to learn to find happiness in less complex things.

Percolating down the ways in which we coped with Covid is challenging. Most of these mechanisms weren't adopted by design, but rather out of necessity, or lack of other options. There are many ways I found to cope throughout the pandemic which we can get into, but I don't think any of them would have been as effective without first developing an important parent strategy – perspective.

There was no explicit choice in finding different ways to cope. These things usually result from whatever your underlying attitude and experience is, don't they? For example, if I took on an attitude of hopelessness, or self-pity, I may not have bothered to exercise as much and I may have drank a lot more alcohol than I did. To me, the foundational attitude is important for developing any potentially useful coping strategies.

Gaining Perspective

It would have been easy, and generally accepted, I imagine, to regress to a mindset of self-pity throughout Covid. After all, many of us had to give up so much of our modern lives in order to weather the storm. I had to cancel a 6 month long trip to South America. It would have been so easy to wallow and sulk and scream **'Poor me!'** but it would not at all have been helpful.

Understanding your own situation within the grand scheme of things helps to put things into perspective. Although I, like many others, had to give up so much of my life, I was in a fairly privileged position, one that I am grateful for. Most pertinent being that I had no underlying health conditions, was young, and generally enjoyed good health and fitness. Covid didn't threaten me the same way it threatened other demographics. The biggest sacrifice I had to make was social – and that is no small thing – but there were far more drastic and terminal sacrifices made throughout the Covid era, and so gaining perspective over where I stood certainly made it far easier to cope. Sure, life didn't look the way I thought it would, but I had a lot to be grateful for. Reminding myself of these things on a regular basis became a very important way to navigate the pandemic.

Perspective in the face of adversity breeds resilience, does it not? Knowing that the road ahead will improve, knowing that things could be far worse for you, and knowing that you have the strength to endure, all help to keep you moving forward. Perspective was key, and it continues to remain key.

Exercise

Even in more precedented times, away from world-bending viruses, I have always leaned on exercise for both my physical and mental health. Exercise seems to me to be the most freely available and most effective form of anti-depressant we have, but it is rarely promoted as such. This is a hill I will die on. And although not everyone can exercise due to a variety of disabilities and other factors, it is still a form of mental coping that should be suggested to those who can exercise. It is not ableist to suggest that those who can exercise should exercise. Many people cannot afford to go to therapy but this doesn't prevent us from suggesting that people go if possible. Both exercise and therapy work, and so if you have the means, you should actively utilise these coping mechanisms.

Our bodies are designed for movement. Our limbs are made for stretching and walking and exploring. They are not designed to be sitting down for the majority of the day, but our modern lifestyle has made this a reality. Exercise is often regarded as difficult, unnecessary and taxing when really it is our default mode of being. The rush of endorphins, and other neurotransmitters like dopamine and serotonin associated with strenuous exercise improves various aspects of mental health (Mikkelsen et al., 2017). However, exercise is rarely referenced as a mental health tool despite its effectiveness.

Throughout the pandemic, with gyms closed and basketball courts forbidden zones, I did the one thing I swore I'd never do – I started running. The cursed, most honest form of exercise imaginable. There are no places to hide. You just have to run and sweat and feel your knees bulge and your calves scream and your thighs ache. For my whole life I've been surrounded by career runners. Fellas who ran competitively in school and who often competed in races and marathons. Masochists from where I was standing. I believed these people just enjoyed running. It was not a painful endeavour for them, but rather gave them the same joy that basketball had always given me. But I was wrong about this, too.

For most of the pandemic I lived with one of these career runners. He ran six days a week, every week, without fail. When I confronted him about this madness I assumed it was something he enjoyed. So you can imagine my shock when he told me that no one who runs enjoys the actual act of running. It's not the act where the reward lies. It's battling that little voice in your head that tells you to stop running. It's running long and hard as far as you possibly can, despite the pain. The reward is in the discipline. It's in dominating the self. The endorphins that come after a run are unlike anything else in any other form of exercise I've ever engaged with. And I think this is because you can't take breaks, or go easy, or cheat. It's honest work for honest pay, and there's a lot to be said for it.

So, I traded lifting weights and shooting jump shots for running out of necessity during the pandemic. Exercise has always been a huge crutch for me in life. It kept me going when I was depressed in college and it acts as a constant when life is uncertain and confusing. I often wonder how different and more challenging my life would be without exercise being so bloody prominent. Since then, all the way back in 2020, I've kept up the running despite my reluctance and now I can't imagine a life without running. At the time of writing I've now completed my first marathon, which is something I never thought I'd be able to say.

It's weird how these things happen. Despite the pandemic and Covid being such a tumultuous time, there were many positive things that emerged from it for all of us. We just rarely take the time to appreciate them because we're trained to only focus on the negatives from a very young age.

Embrace the Chaos

Life is short. Time seems to speed up the older you get. I remember when summers used to feel everlasting as a child. More recently summers go by in the blink of an eye. We have very little control over how our lives will go despite our efforts. Life happens and we bare witness.

A meteor might strike the Earth. A(nother) deadly virus could break out. Nuclear war is a very real threat. Anything could happen and there's nothing we can do about it. This can be a scary idea but it can also be quite a liberating one. In an world where the future is uncertain, it pays to live directly and exclusively in the present.

ESSAYS ON COVID-19

In the beginning, like everyone else, I tuned in. I watched the news. I kept track of the daily numbers, both of cases and sadly, of deaths. I was fixated on this one thing which wreaked havoc and induced fear and controlled. Covid was and is real, but it doesn't necessarily have to control us. Life, no matter what is going on in the rest of the world, is fleeting. Our limited minutes slip away regardless of an ongoing pandemic or not. At a certain point I realised this, and I stopped tuning in. I stopped watching the news and I stopped living in fear. I followed rules when necessary but I switched off from the fear-mongering and propaganda. I lived as close to my normal life as I could and I stopped worrying about the future. Hypothetical 'what if' thinking only leads to worrying, and worrying does nothing but destroy the present moment.

Eventually, we crawled out from under the fear collectively. Not all of us, but we've learned to live with Covid a bit more effectively. Vaccines and placebo effects help. They always have. I was even able to travel around Europe for 9 weeks at one stage and I never managed to be captured by the virus. No matter what is happening out there, life goes on. Sometimes the angry people inside our phones try to convince us otherwise.

We all want to be part of a tribe. It's in our genetic make-up. A longing to belong. In the beginning of the pandemic it felt good to be part of the blindly led majority. We were all in it together, after all. However, as time went on rules and lockdowns began to make less sense. Studies began to showcase their efficacy or lack thereof

(Herby et al., 2022). People conformed out of fear rather than because rules actually made sense and worked. Pantomimes were allowed to go ahead but children couldn't attend. It was impossible to spread Covid within schools. There was nonsense everywhere.

It was within these moments that I truly found that overarching mechanism to cope: Perspective. The world would spin on in chaos. Wrapped in division and anger and uncertainty. And yet, none of it was obligatory. We all had a choice. We could either allow the external madness to seep within and cause us to panic, and to become anxious and bitter and sad. Or we could do what the Stoics, all those years ago, taught us to do. We could stop the external from affecting the internal. We could focus only on that which was in our immediate control and ignore anything outside of it. We could understand that the world will forever be in chaos while simultaneously learning to exist outside of it.

Pandemics come and go. History has shown us that. There is always something else to fill the void. War. Famine. Climate crisis. These things will never go away. They will always happen. The struggle is part of what it means to be alive. Sisyphus, in the iconic myth, pushed a rock up a hill for eternity (Camus, 1955). To live is to struggle. We must find ways to exist in this reality, and for me, this means focusing on what is within my control.

It's not that we should ignore the harsh reality of our world, but rather we must find ways to live well despite it. After all, as Camus famously said, one must imagine Sisyphus happy.

References

Aurelius, M. (2013). *Marcus Aurelius: Meditations, Books 1-6.* Oxford University Press.

Camus, A. (1955). The Myth of Sisyphus. 1942. *Trans. Justin O'Brien.*

Herby, J., Jonung, L., & Hanke, S. (2022). A Literature Review and Meta-Analysis of the Effects of Lockdowns on COVID-19 Mortality. *Studies in Applied Economics*, (200).

Mikkelsen, K., Stojanovska, L., Polenakovic, M., Bosevski, M., & Apostolopoulos, V. (2017). Exercise and mental health. *Maturitas, 106*, 48-56.

Embracing a Positive Mindset During Covid-19

Jennifer Murphy

Introduction

For the duration of my adult life, I have held a deep interest in the power of positive mindset, the phenomenon of resilience and the skills required to remain focused on desired results, regardless of current circumstances. Not unlike most people, there have been ample opportunites in my life to test this theory when faced with scenarios one considers less than ideal. The recent and ongoing COVID-19 pandemic has generated a reset like no other to date, in the 21st Century. A global reshuffle of priorities, expectations and demands on both professional and personal experiences has occurred.

Having spent over a decade as a Human Resource Practitioner, I genuinely thought I had seen it all. In my role, I deal with all aspects of the employee lifecycle within an organisation, which in and of itself requires an ability to connnect, build a raport and cultivate relationships with vast numbers of people. Often, situations give rise to a deeper understanding or knowledge of an employee's personal life when external circumstances impact their ability to perform in their role.

Broadly speaking, pre-pandemic, my key objectives were focused upon the strategic positioning of human capital to ensure effective and consistent implementation of practices which deliver overall organisational goals. The priviledge from my perspective, is to have input at a senior strategic level within which, my decisions bear influence upon the organisational culture and contribute to the ultimate overall performance.

Hospitality is a unique industry, an 'acquired taste' some might say. The grand buildings and impressive dining outlets, exquisite bedrooms and luxurious spas draw guests from far and wide to rest, relax and rejuvenate and disconnect from their ordinary day to day lives. A place where all life events are celebrated and memories are made. Like the industry itself, the hospitality professional is also a certain type of individual. In previous articles (Murphy, 2021), I have discussed in detail, the characteristics of hospitality workers but, to briefly summarise, hospitality workers are generally intrinsically motivated individuals who find purpose and meaning in their work through service. The 'rewards' for hospitality professionals are, quite often, the smiles and positive feedback from the guest. Having an opportunity to positvely impact the experience of another is what ultimately drives this cohort of worker (Chiang and Shawn Jang, 2008; Louden, 2012) Assisting a nervous partner with the orchestration of a surprise proposal, planning the weddings of thousands of starry eyed couples, celebrating life's milestones and significant birthdays and assisting a bereft family with sensitive arrangements after the passing of a loved one.

Life Happens in Hotels

Life happens in hotels. The teams who plan, organise and execute the aforementioned, play a role not only as an employee but as a creator of memorable experiences that can last a lifetime. Many guests have taken time to write thank you cards or send emails to Senior Management to highlight employees for their exceptional care and attention. I am confident that any leader would agree, the sheer joy expressed by team members when acknowledged in this manner is wonderful to witness and rewarding beyond measure. These are the golden moments that offset the gross disparity in remuneration when compared to other similar operational roles in comparible tertiary industries, the unsociable hours and often unattractive tasks. People are what Hospitality is made of, in the absence of genuine service providers, the guest experience becomes dull, robotic and functional.

How can Hospitalitly function in a pandemic? How do we engage and connect with our people when we don't see them for weeks and months on end? These were the questions posited by Human Resource professionals in recent times. While some properties made the decision to remain open for essential workers or offer their vacant property as a quarantine facility, others had no alternative but to close the doors and bid farewell to their hard working teams, promising to keep in touch whilst simultaneously wondering how long a calander of virtual events could keep a team united.

I recall the eerie feeling of walking around an empty hotel, looking at vast spaces that would ordinarily be crammed with guests chatting and enjoying themselves while staff tended to their every need in the hope of creating a wonderful and memorable experience. As I climbed the magnificent staircase to work in isolation from a meeting room, a sense of dread quickly set in, as the reality of the uncertainty which lay ahead began to unravel in my mind. While I was incredibly appreciative of the opportunity to remain in employment, I was also anxious about my team and the impact of temporary lay off for them both personally and professionally. For myself, I had to reassess my activities.

Disconnection

Ordinarily, my role is quite disconnected from the team in that I work primarily with the Executive Team whilst coaching and supporting the individual Department Managers. It is a very rare circumstance that would find me dealing directly with a team member, as it is my belief that managers should be empowered to manage their own teams effectively whilst being supported behind the scenes. This approach has proved successful in the past and creates autonomy for the manager and a culture of trust and professional development. During lockdown, not all managers were working as some chose to stay home and use the time to be with family or explore other interests which meant I became the point of contact for all staff queries and concerns.

While it was my role to keep the team motivated and upbeat, I will admit that I found this at times exhausting particularly on days when I was feeling anxious myself about my own family and life situation. Being an introverted person, with a limited circle of close friends I suddenly found myself physically alone yet "virtually" surrounded by people via phone, email, and video calls. In order to maintain a level of calm in this overwhelming scenario, namely being the point of contact for over 200 people, often accessible long after the working day officially ended, frequently dealing with team members personal stress and worry, I needed to find new levels of resilience and strength to pull myself through the uncertainty. I wanted to be able to distance my own emotions from the circumstances of others, whilst still remaining supportive and helpful so that I could be present for my own family and show up for my team.

I became acutely aware that the self-care advice I was abundantly offering to everyone around me, was indeed lacking in my own life. I realised I had forgotten to mind myself while desperately trying to keep everyone connected and upbeat. In order to address this, I did what I do best, in a situation of stress; I withdrew, turned my attention inward, I stepped myself out of the chaos and into mindfulness practices. Starting off slowly, with simple things such as taking deep conscious breaths or interrupting a spiralling negative thought pattern by changing my body's position, focusing on grounding myself, and using gratitude as the basis for my thoughts, I became much more connected with myself and less absorbed with my mind activity and projections of an impossible to predict future.

Daily Self-Care

Having always been an active member of the gym and regularly practicing meditation, I found it most helpful to revert back to this as a daily prescription of self-care. I increased the intensity and frequency of my fitness regime and committed to spending at least fifteen minutes a day meditating and enjoying grounding exercises.

As a result of my increased exercise, I made healthier food choices and spent more time outside in the fresh air regardless of the weather. I also enjoy academic writing and during the stressful periods I found solace and peace in journaling and writing. The focus required for me to write, literally became all-consuming and acted as a portal for me to escape to another world. I still became concerned when I saw rising case numbers especially within the vicinity of my home, however, I was much better equipped to respond to negative media coverage and the constant barrage of case numbers, clusters and the sadness of lives lost not to mention the ever-evolving mutations offering a new threat.

Once the official Government announcement was delivered, and Hospitality was permitted to reopen fully in June 2021, the joy of having people back in the building was extraordinary. The collective positive energy was tangible. Our guests were ready to enjoy the property again and our team welcomed them back. As business levels skyrocketed and life returned to somewhat normal, there was another twist in the Coronavirus tale for the Human Resource Department. As interaction levels increased in the operation, and the world reopened, the reality of increasing case numbers once again re-emerged.

Antigen testing was one of our best forms of defence to keep our team and our guests safe. While testing staff could never be unilaterally mandated, it was encouraged, and free tests were made available to all. At this point, it was determined that HR was best placed to manage the testing of team members due to the sensitivity of the situation. I was not prepared for the fact that I would be physically conducting the nasal swabbing and delivering results to highly anxious, often tearful team members. The HR Department for all intents and purposes became a rapid test centre. Increasing levels of anxiety among the team whipped around the building as we endeavoured to fire-fight the tidal wave of cases relentlessly presenting on an hourly basis. Remaining focused as we negotiated the impact of almost entire departments moving to isolation at various stages of the outbreaks was only a secondary challenge compared to avoiding a potentially life-threatening virus.

Managing the information which needed to be reliably reported to the health authorities was also a new area of learning and required an unforeseen level of investigation to ensure all close contacts were traced accurately and contacted. All of this was happening behind closed doors in a fully occupied hotel where the guest experience could not be impaired. Once again, it was the inner peace and calm of mindfulness and physical exercise that gave me the resilience to keep going despite the fact that I felt my role was now entirely unrecognisable.

Conclusion

Mindfulness practices, a deep sense of appreciation for life, academic writing and physical exercise became significant parts of my daily routine. It is my belief that these activities contributed substantially to my overall mental and physical health, and are the reason I successfully avoided contracting COVID-19 despite my work placing me at the centre of every surge the property encountered. I am deeply grateful for every day, for the people in my life and the good health to continue to live in the present moment.

References

Chiang, C. and (Shawn) Jang, S. (2008). An expectancy theory model for hotel employee motivation. International Journal of Hospitality Management, 27(2), pp.313-322.

Louden, K., (2012). 'Preventing Employee Turnover'. Collector, 78(2), pp. 39-40.

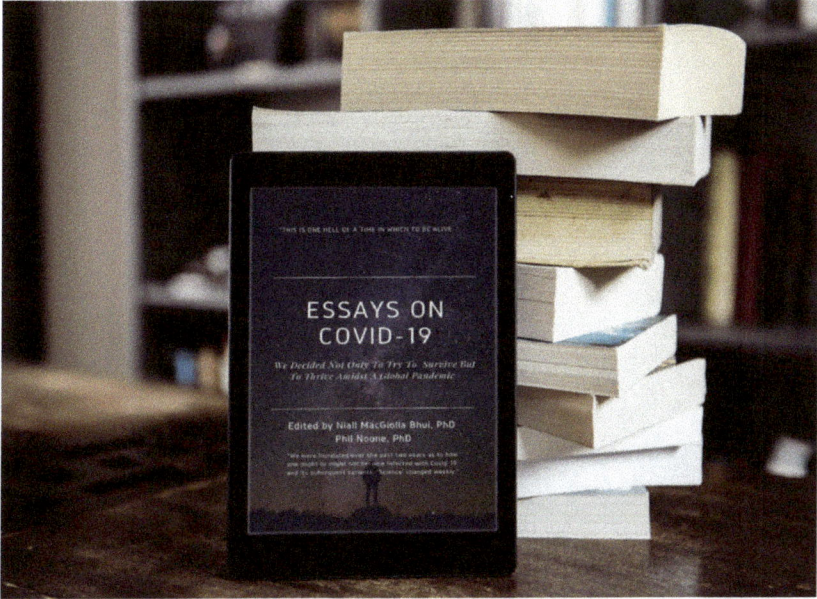

'Look! People!' Finding My Light in the Pandemic

Karen Gallen

'Look! People!'

Despite all the 'new' words and phrases introduced throughout the world through all forms of media arising from Covid-19, 'Look! People!' will forever be etched in my personal experience of lockdown. To give some background, I should explain that on 7th March, 2020 my daughter, aged 12 at the time, left Temple Street Children's Hospital in Dublin, Ireland following spinal surgery. She has additional physical needs and a moderate to severe learning disability, plus severe scoliosis. Her early discharge was 'allowed' by her surgeon on my request due to the increasing reporting of Covid-19 cases and the fear of being in hospital where cases were all too present. Such was the fear of the known/unknown at the time that the Security cleared a path in the corridors of the hospital to facilitate the transfer of a child with a 'suspected' case of Covid-19 from an ambulance to an isolation ward. The fear was real and was driven by the media and public alike.

A government announcement delivered the following week confirmed the closure of schools, and I will admit I felt a sense of relief, as having a medically compromised child made the 'threat' of Covid-19 more menacing for her and, indeed, my family. So began the cocooning process and I kept my daughter indoors for several weeks until such time that cabin fever brought us to our tipping point, and I put her in the car for a local drive. The streets were deserted and eerie and the drive did nothing to lighten the mood between us until we turned a corner, and she heard the laugher of children from a garden. From the stony silence of the back of the car she perked up and shouted, 'Look! People!' To this day, my stomach somersaults when I think about that moment because the crippling loneliness that lockdown brought to many, brought the same loneliness tenfold to a child with additional needs.

'Loneliness and the feeling of being unwanted is the most terrible poverty.'

—Mother Teresa

Lifestyle Changes

Like many others, life changed dramatically when the initial lockdown was imposed in March 2020. Prior to this, my usual day comprised of a school drop at secondary school, school drop at primary school, dash to work, primary school collection at lunchtime, drop to granny's house for childminding during my lunch break, eat in the car, drive home after work, dinners, schoolwork, gym, sleep, repeat. Top this off with medical appointments and therapy visits for my daughter and every minute of my day was accounted for. Suddenly, this all came to a halt, but a different level of frenzy ensued. Granted, it was nice to work from home, not commute, set the alarm for an hour later, be 'home' from the office immediately after office hours etc. I initially embraced this new lifestyle and everyone was more relaxed and appreciative of the slower pace of life. However, like most things, the honeymoon period was short and the stark implications of restrictions hit home. No household visits, no lunches with friends, no after school activities, no, no, no, no – almost every word had a no before it. The only word at that time that I wanted to put 'no' before was Covid.

After an unusually quiet dinnertime one Sunday, I asked my 14-year-old son if everything was okay? He had been 'coping' so well with the restrictions, however, all was not as it seemed. He was too upset to reply initially but his dinner plate literally filled with tears and, after ten minutes of sobbing, he said, 'I'm so sick of this. It's like being in prison.' His outburst of emotions triggered the same in me. I came to the realisation that everyone was experiencing a loss and my youngest child who has additional needs lost out on so much and continues to do so.

While children and teenagers missed physical meet-ups with their peers, they continued to have interaction with their friends, through online gaming, Snapchat, Microsoft Teams etc. but for a child with an intellectual disability, or in my daughter's case both an intellectual and physical disability, these forms of communication are not suitable. Her social life/playdates/friends were all school-based and when school closed, so did her options to have friends or interaction with friends. This was a harsh and unwelcome new reality. It was a time of loss on so many levels. For me also, there was a loss as my independence from the house suffered, yet somehow I also made some gains. Gains I hear you say! Yes, I gained the somewhat dubious titles of 'working from home colleague', 'teacher', 'friend', 'speech therapist', 'physiotherapist', 'occupational therapist' to name but some. I had to assume all of those roles to maintain some 'normality' for my daughter as all-face-to face appointments were cancelled.

'Beautiful days do not come to you. You must walk towards them.'
—Rumi

Hospital

Attending hospital is a daunting process for most people but attending hospital during a pandemic was a surreal experience. My daughter had recent surgeries in March 2020, October 2020, April 2021 and November 2021. Each experience was different based on the number of Covid cases reported at that time and the level of restrictions that were in place. One visit required a copy of her hospital letter for admittance to the hotel we stayed in the night prior to surgery, as Dublin along with Donegal was on a higher level of restrictions. The hospital appointment letter was also used to pass through a Garda Checkpoint on the motorway when inter-county travel was prohibited. Those were the initial 'challenges' and then came the requirement for a negative PCR test before she could be admitted as a patient. A nasal swab is required for children under 13 and when it was being done I had to hold my breath for fear of what she may say to the Community Swabber. It was not her finest moment. This was a difficult test for her as she has limited movement in her neck. However their patience was endless at the test centre.

You can imagine my delight (sarcasm intended) when, after having received a negative PCR test, her surgery was postponed. Another trip had to be arranged to the test centre the following week (72 hours before surgery) and we were welcomed back – I am convinced that they thought we visited again for the two free face masks and packet of pocket tissues that each person getting tested receives.

Other

School or should I say 'no school' was one of the biggest setbacks for my daughter. She is very sociable and as I previously stated, school was where she flourished socially. Because of her additional needs she does not have the capacity for Microsoft Teams learning but she was extremely fortunate to have the most fabulous teacher. Her teacher drove to the house every Monday to drop off schoolwork for her to do, and every Friday she called with a treat which was always relevant to the week. During a very sunny spell of weather she dropped ice pops for everyone in the house. Another time she brought a bucket and spade. Those socially distanced visits were a highlight of the week for my daughter.

When schools reopened for students, I continued with home-schooling and the teacher would FaceTime my daughter, send cards in the post, and she even Zoom called prior to the Christmas school holidays with a surprise appearance on the call from Santa. As with everything in life, with the good comes the bad. Zoom exhaustion, fatigue, and relentless Covid data reporting took its toll. Sleep patterns were disrupted and every time an occasion such as a family birthday was missed out on, another difficult day was had. The ultimate low of my lockdown was the death of my aunt who tested positive with Covid. Restrictions meant that I watched her funeral online and after driving to the graveyard, I was told that a person needed a pass to enter the graveyard and that passes were also limited.

'I would love to live like a river flows, carried by the surprise of its own unfolding.'

—John O'Donohue, Benedictus

Finding Light in the Darkness

Although there were multiple difficult and challenging periods (including the cancellation of a long planned girls trip to New York), I must say that I learned to appreciate my environment more. I walked almost every day with my best friend, which was a therapy in itself. Initially, we were so fearful of meeting other walkers that we walked at 6.30AM in the morning and on occasion when we encountered another walker, he/she would 'avoid us like the plague' – pardon the pun. I have witnessed many people take a sudden move from the footpath to the road to avoid another pedestrian without giving thought to the possibility of getting knocked down.

I laughed a lot on those walks, and it brought reassurance that some normality remained present. I reignited my love for books but varied the genres I read (from fiction to psychological thrillers to philosophy) and I attempted to grow a veggie patch in my city garden. Surprisingly this was successful – not enough to feed a family but it gave me a sense of accomplishment in a time of uncertainty. I guess for me, I have had a love/hate relationship with lockdowns.

Allow me to finish using a line from a writer I have come to adore over this Covid-19 period where he evocatively writes of blessings. I have many blessings in my life. All of us do if we can just look to them, embrace them, live and love them.

'May you be blessed with good friends, and learn to be a good friend to yourself, Journeying to that place in your soul where, there is love, warmth and feeling. May this change you.'

From 'Benedictus'

Reference

O'Donohue, J. (2007). Benedictus. Transworld Publishing.

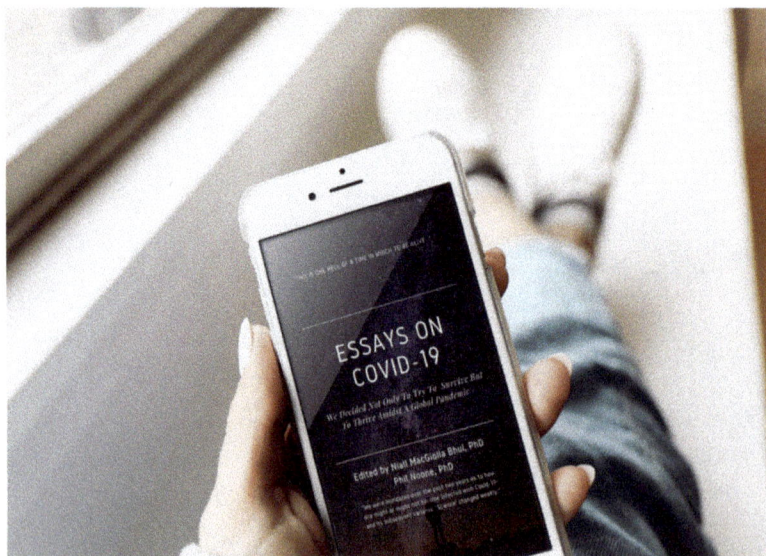

It Takes an Online Village to Survive: New Parenthood in a Global Pandemic

Rachael Hussey

Isolation is a common symptom of motherhood, particularly for new mothers and it is not talked about enough. In these early years before school, you are your child's whole world and *your* whole world has been turned on its head. Many mothers find they lose at least part of their identity, confidence, self-worth, and all-too-often they can no longer identify with their pre-child self. Your whole lifestyle changes drastically and with each new baby you have to adapt and create a new normal. It can feel like the world is going on around you while you are standing still.

Covid-19 only added to these already challenging feelings by creating even more distance between a new mother and the rest of the world. New mothers have experienced worryingly high rates of distress during the Covid-19 pandemic, which some link partly to social distancing measures (Taylor 2021). Maternal mental health is particularly important to consider, due to the increased risk for depression and anxiety. Pregnancy and the postpartum period, especially for first time mothers, have been identified as delicate periods in a woman's life that are accompanied by significant social, psychological and also physiological changes and, for this reason, pregnant women have been considered a high-risk population. (Vismara 2021)

My first-time mum experience was pre-covid and as lonely as it was, especially with all our family living a few hours away, I combatted the loneliness over time through getting involved in baby classes, local mom groups, meeting for coffees when I had the stamina and opportunity. Between feeds and naps and exhaustion from being up all night, there often isn't a lot of time and energy for socialising, but when you get the opportunity, it really boosts your mood and you feel more connected.

The feeling of loneliness can be very strong. My second time having a baby was so vastly different to my first experience and all those crutches I leaned on were unavailable. I had to get inventive to survive life with a newborn and a 2.5 year old at home day in day out with no outlets and a husband who was working outside of the home. My only adult interactions were in the evening as an exhausted, weary, hormonal mother were with a tired, drained, overwhelmed Dad, alongside the occasional medical appointment or supermarket journey.

Like many mothers, with my first child I put my everything in to being the 'perfect mum' to the detriment of myself. As a first-time mum, I battled with post-natal anxiety; I worried about everything. I had a challenging infant who cried a lot and fought her naps as many do, and as the months of colic continued, my anxieties did as well. Of course, the lack of sleep made my anxiety soar and with that, the more anxious I was, the less I could sleep. So, even when she would eventually nod off, I lay there paralysed unable to catch 40 winks before the next wake up. The most viscous cycle that I seemed unable to break from.

I put so much pressure on myself to do it all and to be perfect every minute of the day. Activities, stimulation, enough naps, enough socialising, enough classes, enough breast milk, organic homemade food, the right clothes, and yet I never felt enough. I went to the doctor at 4 months postpartum for nausea. I had it for over a month and had no idea what was causing it. My lovely doctor saw something in me that day. She gave me medicine for reflux to see if it helped and she asked me how I was feeling, in detail, not just surface level. Like many women in that situation, I said I was 'fine'. Signs to watch out for in post-natal depression such as not bonding, not wanting to look after the infant, feeling detached and not getting up and out can be very different to post-natal anxiety. I was having the opposite experience, so it did not dawn on me that my anxiety was fielding this perfectionist behaviour and I was incredibly burnt out physically and mentally.

I loved my baby so much but I was pushing impossible standards on myself. Once I was able to open up and explain how I was feeling the doctor listened and just supported me. I started post-natal therapy soon after and I started to loosen the reins, let people help more, realised my intrusive thoughts didn't have to control me, that I was a great mother but that I mattered as well, and that perfection is not possible. I found more balance and I was able to enjoy the fruits of my labour. Motherhood was as hard as it ever was but I was adapting.

By the time Covid-19 began, I had just celebrated my daughter's 2nd birthday and we were really in the swing of parenthood. She had a thriving social life with some little friends and we attended classes and play groups and I worked freelance so she was at home with me 6 days a week. On other day I juggled work around her naps and when my husband had a few free hours. Life was hectic but I was so excited for the future. I felt I had the best of both worlds, albeit not much time for myself or rest, but who does?

Initially in March 2020 when Covid-19 took hold of our world I was terrified. I was in early pregnancy with a toddler and a husband who was in a close contact job role and travelling for work. Everything was so unknown and scary. I was terrified to even go to the doctor's office and there wasn't a hand sanitiser to be found.

ESSAYS ON COVID-19

My husband is a professional rugby player, so his job is demanding physically, but he is also away regularly so our home life is already different to most with so much time away from home resulting in a lot of time parenting on my own. My husband ended up getting surgery on his leg as we entered lockdown and after that he had to train from home. While he was recovering it was hellish, but when he had healed and was again able to help his pregnant wife with our 2 year old, it ended up being a magical time for us all.

Before Covid-19 my only experience as a parent was spending a lot of time with my daughter on my own as my husband travelled every 2 weeks for games and weekends were spent playing matches, from April to June 2020, we were all together in the house full time having so much time together was amazing, especially while I was pregnant. I had time to rest and while our daughter napped for a couple of hours, I could even do some yoga, eat, and watch some TV. It really was a special time. Of course, I was uncomfortable and exhausted and very busy with an extremely active toddler but having support there during that time was something I will never forget.

That time, of course, did not last forever and when he returned to in-house training in July and back to games and travel, that is when Covid-19 life started to get more challenging for me yet again. While his life returned to normal, I was still crazily busy with our 2 year old. Thankfully, this period was when government enforced restrictions lifted somewhat, so I was able to see family a little bit but with Covid in that first stage, we also had to be very careful. With Matthew's job, a lot of the time we couldn't have people in our house as we had to limit his contacts for work so that he could test negatively. As my pregnancy progressed, even simple things like a midwife's check-up were very challenging as I would be given set days and times and was unable to bring my toddler, yet we were not supposed to mingle with other households and Matthew was not always free from work at that time.

Without the classes and toddler groups and meeting friends with kids, I thought Sophia Lily would suffer but, at that stage, she seemed more than happy to have my full attention and enjoyed our nature walks around our area and our busy days around the house. I was lonely, of course, but overall it was manageable with eased restrictions.

That all changed in late October 2020 when I gave birth to our beautiful second daughter Mila Rose and we entered an initially short 6 week lockdown with a few weeks ease up over December and then a long, strict, winter lockdown that nearly broke me with my newborn and toddler. Unable to see anyone, dark mornings and evenings, no restaurants open, and only takeaway available in our Wild West winter, it was a dark time figuratively and literally.

Challenges of early motherhood alongside a husband travelling and working and no company, led me to feel extremely isolated and lonely.

The challenges of life with a newborn with feeding issues and a toddler who was struggling massively with no longer being my entire universe, and a husband who continued to leave for work every day and travel, and no outside interactions led me to feel extremely isolated and lonely. I imagined taking the girls to baby and toddler groups, or soft play to tire my older baby out so she would take a long nap while I sat with my newborn, coffees with mom friends and help from family. None of that was possible. I felt robbed of what I envisioned for this transitional period from a family of 3 to 4. Of course we were prepared for all the challenges but to not have any outlets for your child, nor company or help for myself made things incredibly difficult. The classic phrase toted around of, 'It takes a village to raise a child' is very true and in recent years we have become aware that the traditional lifestyle of raising a family with a tight knit community and multigenerational households, is not the reality for most families nowadays. With the popularity of the nuclear family and capitalism as strong as ever, parenthood has become much more isolating and exhausting.

Covid-19 has exasperated this to an extreme level and with children under the age of 3 even more so! 'In the absence of the village, we're disadvantaged like never before. We may have more freedoms than our foremothers, but our burden remains disproportionately, oppressively heavy.' (Berry, 2022) While dealing with extreme loneliness and overwhelm and spending a lot of time on my couch nursing my newborn, I gravitated towards the online world. For a lot of us, the internet made all the lockdowns bearable, the opportunity to connect with friends and family virtually as well as follow strangers and celebrities who might be experiencing the same things as us was a lifeline. Where we could no longer do this in our community and with our loved ones, we could now connect with people perhaps thousands of miles away, the collective experience we were all having regardless of our background, socioeconomic position, age or gender, allowed us all to be much more vulnerable and to relate more to each other. People were more willing to open up online and to be emotional. I think it was a really beautiful result.

For me as a young mother with infants, when I had a particularly challenging day, I could check a mum influencer's Instagram story and see what mishaps she was facing that day with her little ones. I could scroll TikTok when I had 5 minutes and get an instant boost and a laugh from some comedic skits of the chaos of small children. Desperate for human contact and connection, social media became my saving grace!

This moment in time with its very specific nuances is hard to articulate, yet any of us who experienced it can probably relate. Of course, having physical support and interaction with people and other mothers would have been much more helpful but the online experience allowed me to feel less alone and to feel as I was still a part of something. When you don't have the time to contact everyone, the opportunity to post a few stories of you and your kids and watching others doing the same helps our connection and is less exhausting, too.

While our first lockdown was bathed in warm, dry, long days, the later ones were much more challenging for most due to the weather and short days, and we were all so burnt out and exhausted from the pandemic by this stage. The first lockdown was met with mutterings of 'thank God this is during spring and summer and the beautiful weather; can you imagine doing this in winter?' No one could have prepared us for just how long the pandemic lasted. I truly don't know how I would have survived the isolation of my husband working outside the home and travelling abroad with a newborn and 2 year old without social media and our smart phones. FaceTime, WhatsApp, Instagram and eventually TikTok, became my lifelines and my solace. Nowadays with a 1.5 year old and a 4 year old, I am just as busy but I'm no longer scrolling with one arm while breastfeeding on the couch, with Peppa Pig playing for my toddler or getting nap trapped under a sleepy newborn. I now have much less time again to spend online.

While now I am running around after a 1 and 4 year old, I am no longer spending much time scrolling social media but in between chores and snack duties, I enjoy catching up and watching a quick skit on Tik-Tok regarding the joys of early parenthood. It still helps me feel connected in a world that is less community based.
Running around after a 1 year old does not leave much space for that but I still enjoy stealing a few minutes while preparing a snack

or emptying the dishwasher to check in and grab a few laughs from a mum who explains what it's like getting her 2 toddlers ready to leave the house with impeccable comedic timing and some clever wit, still helps me feel less alone. I think with the 'village' long gone; we are now creating our own village through supporting parents online. You can still get stuck on the wrong side of the *'Pinterest mums'* or the very aesthetically pleasing accounts that make out parenthood and family life to be like an easy dream without showing the real, raw, hard truths and I now shy away from that. Comparison is the thief of joy as they say. I think the future is in uplifting parents and not shying away from the nitty gritty, most of us are trying our absolute best and we have all had an extremely hard two plus years, so why not empower each other instead of shaming and judging? I think the vulnerability we all displayed during these hard times will encourage us to continue to be our more authentic selves and show compassion above all else. At least I hope, while online I have seen more and more accounts slipping back into self-centredness and competitiveness, I encourage everyone to simply click the 'unfollow' and to seek out accounts that inspire us and make us feel seen and heard. I believe doing this saved my sanity (mostly) in an otherwise almost impossible time in my life. I was able to feel a little bit less alone and a little bit more seen. Having my girls see their extended family members and grandparents on a screen, voice-noting my pals and watching funny skits, made the isolation just a little bit easier and, for that, I am forever grateful.

Many of us learned to give ourselves a little more grace and to judge less through Covid and I hope we can continue with that positivity and let go of the idea of *perfection*. The trials we face in testing times are what ultimately strengthen us. It is empowering to acknowledge this in moments of adversity such as this global pandemic that engulfed us all. Let us continue to learn and grow from surviving such a strange time in history.

References

Ahmad, Monica, and Laura Vismara. "The Psychological Impact of Covid-19 Pandemic on Women's Mental Health during Pregnancy: A Rapid Evidence Review." International Journal of Environmental Research and Public Health, MDPI, 2 July 2021, https://www.ncbi.nlm.nih.gov/pmc/articles/PMC8297318/.

Berry, Beth. "In the Absence of 'the Village,' Mothers Struggle Most." Motherly, 27 Apr. 2022, https://www.mother.ly/relationships/community-friendship/in-the-absence-of-the-village-mothers-struggle-most/?amp=1.

Ucl, Dr Billie Lever Taylor et al. "Mums Alone." Psychiatry, 10 Nov. 2021, https://www.ucl.ac.uk/psychiatry/news/2021/nov/mums-alone.

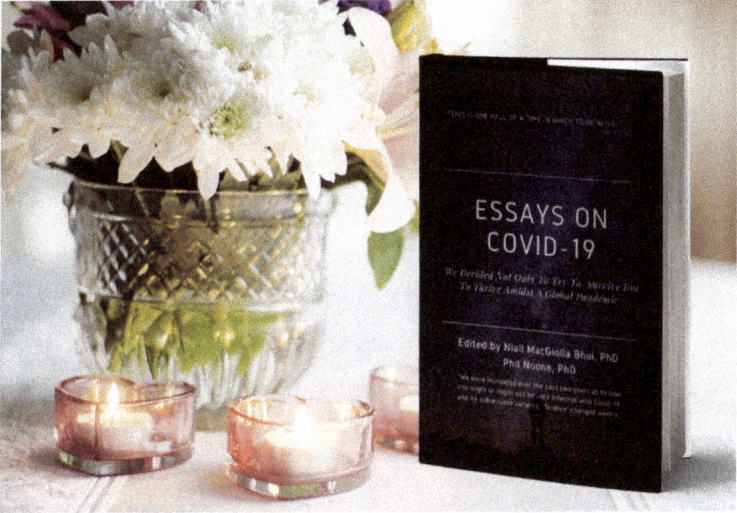

Gardening for the Soul

Susan McKenna

Introduction

There is now a pervasive sense of collective and individual anxiety that our formal health systems either cannot cope with or will not be able cope well into the future. We have both an increasing and ageing population in Ireland and we have, literally, thousands of adults, adolescents and children on waiting lists for medical procedures.

We also understand that our overreliance on pharmaceutical drugs is neither good for governments nor patients as their costs are spiralling and many are less effective than they have been in the past.

Added to this is the very unwelcome side effects of all too many drugs.

This chapter details my holistic interest in horticulture and gardening and how I immersed myself in my own garden over the various lockdowns in 2020 and 2021 brought in by the Irish government. I spent time in nature, outside, feet grounded in the soil, planting and growing. Just me, my hens, my dog, various visiting curious wildlife, the songs of the birds and the open blue sky above me. I have emerged some two years later 'a wiser, deeper woman' to paraphrase the American singer, Johnny Cash.

Health and Wellness

It's worth recognising at the start of the chapter that our *good* health depends on several things including, social, economic and environmental factors. During the height of the Covid-19 pandemic, our GP offices were closed to the public. Our hospitals did not want visitors. Everything moved online. But, outside, nature continued doing what it does, growing all around us. Now, use of 'therapeutic gardens' have been a staple in hospital grounds for thousands of years (Fuller *et al.,* 2007). Nothing new in this. Florence Nightingale advocated their use in the 18th century, noting that patients, visitors and staff all benefit from flowers and shrubs (Lohr *et al.,* 1996; Peacock *et al.,* 2018; Sempik *et al.,* 2003) so I believe I was well intentioned and, at least, somewhat well informed as to what I might do to sustain my own mental health. I even signed up to a horticulture course once restrictions eased. A far cry from my degree in social care practice.

Here's the Science...

The research literature has investigated the health benefits associated with people's engagement with three things; nature, green spaces and the outdoors is well summarised by Pretty et al. (2011) as part of the UK National Ecosystem Assessment (UK National Ecosystem Assessment, 2011) if you're interested in a deep dive into this theme. And, there are many other English language studies from Australia, the USA, Canada, and New Zealand (Kingsley et al., 2009, Draper and Freedman, 2010) that have produced really interesting findings. What is referred to as *horticultural therapy* has been advocated specifically for mental health and a range of mental health programmes (Spurgeon and Underhill, 1979) and this is something I advocated for in my work with at risk youth and families some two decades ago.

Something as simple as smell and colour have a dramatic effect on people's wellbeing, reducing stress. Whilst it is accurate to note that all too few complementary therapies offer convincing data on their effectiveness, this cannot be said for gardening specifically and nature more generally, which most certainly do help us in all sorts of ways. Just read some of the daily social media posts from my colleague Dr. Phil Noone for evidence of this.

Here's something fascinating. Would you believe that several research studies have confirmed that the simple act of even looking at a green space through a window actually relaxes people and reduce their stress? (Ulrich *et al.*, 1993; Unruh, 1984). Pretty et al., (2007) wrote about the restorative effects of working in gardens, the very act of physical exercise in itself is important as a destressor from our day to day lives.

In a more macro context, no surprise, then, that our trees, hedges, and array of plants mitigate, at least to an appreciable extent, climate change which is the scourge of our era and an unwelcome legacy for children and grandchildren. They trap carbon and emit much needed oxygen offsetting as much as 25% of human generated carbon dioxide. Our Ozone is safer (Beard and Green, 1994). It makes sense to get out into our gardens for so many reasons even if we become 'selfish altruists' to borrow a term from my friend, Ammar.

Here's My Response...

This book is about how we responded to Covid-19 – and survived. I'm aware that many people took to baking banana bread, home office exercise and binge watching series on Netflix to cope with the pandemic. This just wasn't for me. I also don't particularly enjoy social media as I find it both distracting and a false environment full of fake (whitened) smiles. So, wellies on, rake in hand, dog by my side, I left the Hub office and ventured out into the Hub garden. There is a simple joy in a dog walking beside you wagging his tail with expectation…

I had first planted groves of birch trees and beech hedging some sixteen years ago so there was a level of maturity around me. I was not working off a blank canvas. But, I had my mind set on my vegetable plot where I had previously planted carrots, peas, onions, broccoli and fruit plants but now saw an opportunity to add more plants to this, such as beetroot, purple broccoli, potatoes and runner beans. This meant preparing the soil in advance to get it in the best condition for the vegetables. Seeds needed to be started indoors so that they were strong and healthy for when they could be transplanted out.

Once planted, the daily battle against pests, diseases and lack of water began. Each stage required a different skill set and required my movement from indoors to outdoors; from artificial light to natural light, from slate flooring in the house to the soil outside. There is significant evidence that this transition is, quite literally, grounding (Fuller et al., 2007). I have found the ability to get lost in another world deeply enriching…but I think my family might disagree with this as I often forget all sense of time and, often, dinner appears on the table a lot later than planned!

Susan McKenna

Here's what I've learned over the past two years since Covid-19 made an appearance. When we plant shrubs and grow flowers, plants and vegetables, we truly engage with our natural world and, crucially, do so at nature's pace and not ours. We are forced to reflect and appreciate growth. We physically witness the seasons change. This is surely the perfect antidote to the all-so-many stresses of (post)modern life and a replacement to prescription drugs. We make ourselves wealthy and not the big pharma companies.

It seems reasonable to argue that our governments could have used the pandemic as an opportunity to heavily promote the notion of active green spaces and alongside these, food growing spaces where our environments are enhanced, where people of all ages are attracted back out into gardens – both public and private. In urban areas, allotments and community food growing initiatives have been hugely successful.

So, in our own little patch of the world, wherever that may be, I would advise you to plant, plant, plant and watch life grow. If this is just a single window box in an apartment, it matters not. If it's an expansive garden, just go for it. Start with what you are most familiar with and then experiment with new flowers and produce. When you get to sit at your table and eat your own home grown delights, your heart will soar. Happy gardening.

References

Beard JB, Green RL. (1994). The role of turfgrasses in environmental protection and their benefits to humans. *J Environ Qual* 1994;23:452–60.

Diette GB, Lechtzin N, Haponik E, Devrotes A, Rubin HR. (2003). Distraction therapy with nature sights and sounds reduces pain during flexible bronchoscopy. *Chest* 2003;123:941–8.

Draper, C. and D. Freedman (2010). Review and Analysis of the Benefits, Purposes, and Motivations Associated with Community Gardening in the United States, Journal of Community Practice, 18:4, 458- 492.

Fuller RA, Irvine KN, Devine-Wright P, Warren PH, Gaston KJ. (2007). Psychological benefits of greenspace increase with biodiversity. *Biol Letters* 2007;3:390–4.

Kingsley, J.Y., Townsend M. and C. Henderson-Wilson (2009). Cultivating health and wellbeing: members' perceptions of the health benefits of a Port Melbourne community garden. Leisure Stud., 28 (2), 207- 219

Lohr VI, Pearson-Mims CH, Goodwin GK. (1996). Interior plants may improve worker productivity and reduce stress in a windowless environment. *J Environ Hort* 1996;14:97–100.

Sempik J, Aldridge J, Becker S. (2003). *Social and therapeutic horticulture: evidence and messages from research.* Loughborough: Centre for Child and Family Research, Loughborough University.

Peacock J, Hine R, Pretty J. (2018). *The mental health benefits of green exercise activities and green care.* MIND, 2007. https://psyk-info. Regionsyddanmark.dk/dwn109161.pdf [Accessed 28th March 2022].

Pretty, J., J. Barton, I. Colbeck, R. Hine, S. Mourato, G. MacKerron and C. Wood (2011). The UK National Ecosystem Assessment Technical Report Chapter 23: Health Values from Ecosystems. In: The UK National

Ecosystem Assessment Technical Report. UK National Ecosystem Assessment, UNEP- WCMC, Cambridge.

Spurgeon, T. and C. Underhill (1979) Horticultural therapy—aspects of land use for the mentally handicapped. A system of planning for the requirements of the mentally handicapped gardener. International Journal of Rehabilitation Research, 2(3), 343-352.

UK National Ecosystem Assessment (2011). The UK National Ecosystem Assessment Technical Report. UNEP-WCMC, Cambridge.

Unruh, A. M. (2004). The meaning of gardens and gardening in daily life: a comparison between gardeners with serious health problems and healthy participants. Acta Hort., 639, 67-73.

Ulrich RS, Lundén O, Eltinge JL. (1993). Effects of exposure to nature and abstract pictures on patients recovering from heart surgery. *Psychphysiol* 1993;Suppl 1:7.

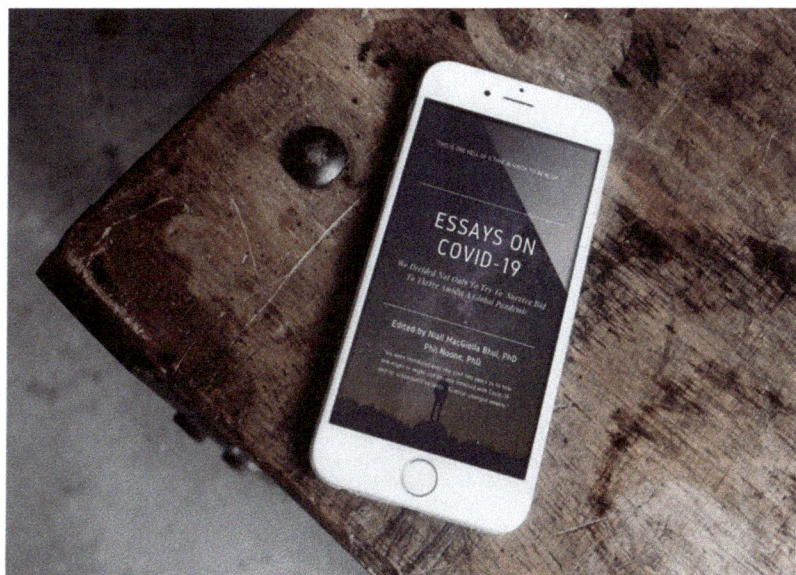

Finding the Joy of Exercise during Covid-19

Anne Hayden

"Take care of your body. It's the only place you have to live."

—Jim Rohn

Correlation between Mental Health and Exercise during Covid

The ongoing Covid-19 pandemic has considerably brought into perspective the effects of isolation and lack of physical activity, and the impacts that these have on the population's mental health. At the same time, the primary focus of this pandemic has been on containing the spread of the disease and preventing mortality (Choi et al., 2020). In the shadow of the Covid-19 crisis, there is a parallel and unprecedented mental health crisis looming (Choi et al., 2020). The impact of Covid-19 on global mental health issues has resulted in an increase in fear, anxiety, growing panic, and a sense of insecurity for oneself and loved ones, as well as depression (Banerjee, 2020). This downturn in peoples' mental health is not just experienced among those staff working in the front line, but also among the general public where there are increasing levels of anxiety reported (MacGiolla Bhuí, 2021). While necessary to stop the spread of the Covid-19 virus, social distancing measures have been found to increase risks for loneliness, isolation, and anxiety among the wider community (Choi et al., 2020). One suggested solution to help lower the effects of the by-products of Covid-19 – anxiety and depression – is to engage in some form of daily exercise activities even from the confines of one's own home (Jurak et al., 2020).

It has been well documented that the relationship between physical health and mental health are closely interwoven (Morrey et al., 2020). In general, in the literature pre-pandemic, it was found that sustained and regular participation in physical activity is associated with positive mental health (McDowell et al., 2019; Schuch et al., 2018; White et al., 2017). A study conducted by Jacob et al. (2020) examined the relationship between exercise and mental health during the pandemic.

Generally, Jacob et al. (2020) found that the number of people with poor mental health, moderate-to-severe depressive symptoms, moderate-to-severe anxiety symptoms, and poor mental wellbeing significantly decreased with increasing physical activity (Jacob et al., 2020). The reasons for this included increases in neurogenesis whereby new neurons are formed in the brain, reductions in inflammatory and oxidant markers, and improvements in self-esteem. However, an interesting note in this study, was that due to the blind study employed, it is not known whether mental health problems lead to lower levels of physical activity or whether lower levels of physical activity lead to mental health problems (Jacob et al., 2020).

The overall findings of this study, suggest that those who have low levels of physical activity during Covid-19 may need to be targeted with support for their mental health going forward. It has previously been acknowledged that, often for many people who are living with a mental illness, exercise is used as a control mechanism; for those without mental illness exercise is used as a protective aspect (Zschucke et al., 2013). However, exercise routines and coping mechanisms have been heavily disrupted by Covid-19.

According to the Economic & Social Research Institute report, Growing Up in Ireland: The Lives of 20-Year-Olds Making the Transition to Adulthood (2021), one in five young Irish men are experiencing symptoms linked to depression, and a third of young Irish women are also experiencing symptoms (O'Mahony et al., 2021). Coupled with this, obesity rates among 20 year olds has seen a sharp increase (O'Mahony et al., 2021). This research suggests that the relationship between young peoples' mental health and attitudes towards exercise needs to be better aligned and prioritised during the continuing Covid-19 pandemic to prevent a future deterioration in public mental health.

Finding an Exercise Routine for me during Covid

Since the first Irish lockdown in March 2020, the way we have had to adapt to life has changed dramatically for us all. The way we live and work has been altered significantly, and we have had to adapt to find a new normal. As part of this adaptation process, the way we spend our time relaxing and dealing with stress has also changed. In early March 2020, pre the Corona Virus, I decided that I needed to make time for self-care and to look after my general health. I had no relationship with exercise, and to say I loathed it would be an understatement. However, I decided to take the bull by the horns and join a gym. This was a very significant departure for me.

I went to my local gym completely daunted by the idea of a signup consultation. Little did I know that during this meeting, I would go on to meet someone who would be instrumental in helping me find a love of exercise and dramatically improve my mental health. On Monday the 9th of March, I joined the gym, and on Thursday the 12th of March, Ireland was placed into a national lockdown and gyms were closed. I could have interpreted this as a sign that exercise simply was not for me; it seemed like the universe was suggesting this. However, during my signup consultation, I was introduced to a personal trainer called Karina, and the following Monday, she sent me a message advising me to take a little walk and to get out and get some air; I would like to say this was a magic lightbulb moment for me with regards to exercise, but it wasn't. Instead slowly, but surely, my stamina and fitness increased through these walks. I found walking integral to getting me out of the house and keeping my spirits up during lockdown.

When restrictions eased and we were allowed to meet outdoors, Karina and I began training together outside in public which was a terrifying prospect as I was not naturally athletic and afraid of the ridicule that I might face by passing members of the public, but in fact no one noticed or cared. Under her and her partner Darragh's guidance, I started weight lifting and resistance training. Every training session, my weights got a little heavier, and I got a little stronger; however, it wasn't until I was a few months into this routine that I noticed I started to see an improvement in both my mental and physical health. My anxiety levels had decreased, my stress levels had reduced, I was noticeably happier and healthier. So much so, that my brother started training also.

During the pandemic, Darragh and Karina took the brave decision to set up a gym called Unlock Fitness which is not a traditional gym; instead of emphasising weight or physical appearance, they focus on health for life and for everyone. This concept of health for all is essential if we as a nation are to take steps to tackle our current mental health crisis, and I think this is the message that we should be spreading to the general public as we adapt to our new normal. I have learned that, like anything worthwhile in life, exercise should be challenging and raise one's heart rate, but it should also be enjoyable and rewarding. We cannot disconnect our physical health from our mental health and vice versa, and while I am not a fitness fanatic by any standards, I do have a newfound respect for both my body and mind, and the connection between the two. So, I will continue to work out three days a week for the foreseeable future and would encourage anyone to find a form of exercise that appeals to them.

References

Banerjee, D., 2020. How COVID-19 is overwhelming our mental health. natindia. https://doi.org/10.1038/nindia.2020.46

Choi, K.R., Heilemann, M.V., Fauer, A., Mead, M., 2020. A Second Pandemic: Mental Health Spillover From the Novel Coronavirus (COVID-19). J Am Psychiatr Nurses Assoc 26, 340–343. https://doi.org/10.1177/1078390320919803

Jacob, L., Tully, M.A., Barnett, Y., Lopez-Sanchez, G.F., Butler, L., Schuch, F., López-Bueno, R., McDermott, D., Firth, J., Grabovac, I., Yakkundi, A., Armstrong, N., Young, T., Smith, L., 2020. The relationship between physical activity and mental health in a sample of the UK public: A cross-sectional study during the implementation of COVID-19 social distancing measures. Mental Health and Physical Activity 19, 100345. https://doi.org/10.1016/j.mhpa.2020.100345

Jurak, G., Morrison, S.A., Leskošek, B., Kovač, M., Hadžić, V., Vodičar, J., Truden, P., Starc, G., 2020. Physical activity recommendations during the coronavirus disease-2019 virus outbreak. J Sport Health Sci 9, 325–327. https://doi.org/10.1016/j.jshs.2020.05.003

Morrey, L.B., Roberts, W.O., Wichser, L., 2020. Exercise-related Mental Health Problems and Solutions during the COVID-19 Pandemic. Curr Sports Med Rep 19, 194–195. https://doi.org/10.1249/JSR.0000000000000725

O'Mahony, D., McNamara, E., Murray, A., Smyth, E., Watson, D., 2021. Growing Up in Ireland: The Lives of 20-Year-Olds — Making the Transition to Adulthood.

Anne Hayden

Zschucke, E., Gaudlitz, K., Ströhle, A., 2013. Exercise and Physical Activity in Mental Disorders: Clinical and Experimental Evidence. J Prev Med Public Health 46, S12–S21. https://doi.org/10.3961/jpmph.2013.46.S.S12

About the Authors

Dr. Niall MacGiolla Bhuí was founding editor of the Irish Journal of Applied Social Studies and editor-in-chief at that journal for a decade. He has travelled extensively lecturing and presenting workshops in Ireland, Northern Ireland, Northern Ireland, England, Sweden and coast to coast Canada. Niall is series co-editor, along with Dr. Phil Noone, of the seven book series, Mental Health For Millennials (published by Book Hub Publishing 2017-2023).

He is also founder and editor of the #ExploringConnectedness book series published by TheDocCheck.Com and the co-editor of this book also published by TheDocCheck.Com. He has authored three books and co-authored another ten books with colleagues across various mental health and humanities themes. Niall currently ghostwrites for a range of national and international clients and mentors Masters and Doctoral candidates across the university sector. His second book of poetry will be published in 2023.

Dr Phil Noone is a Mindfulness Coach/Lecturer with a nursing background who has travelled and worked extensively abroad in a variety of health and well-being settings. She holds an MSc in Mindfulness Based Interventions, a Diploma in Mindfulness and Positive Psychology, a PhD in Sociology and an MSc in Health

Promotion. Phil has lectured for many years at the School of Nursing and Midwifery, University of Galway, and has presented at conferences in South America, Holland, Australia and Ireland. Phil is series co-editor and chapter contributor along with Dr Niall MacGiolla Bhuí of the Mental Health for Millennial Series (1-7), has published papers and conducted research on the themes of 'home', 'well-being', 'rural ageing', 'resilience', 'environmental action and sustainability' and 'Mindfulness'. She has recently set up her own business 'Ocean Mindfulness', delivering Mindfulness at corporate and community level.

Daragh Fleming is an author from Cork in Ireland who uses a conversational style to delve into complex themes which emerge in everyday life. He runs an award-nominated mental health blog and is active voice for mental health in Ireland, delivering talks in a variety of schools, universities and work places. He has two collections of short stories published by Riversong Books, as well as two poetry pamphlets published. His most recent pamphlet, Poems That Were Written On Trains But Weren't Written About Trains was released in July of 2022. His debut in nonfiction - Lonely Boy - arrives with Book Hub Publishing in November 2022.

Anne Hayden is a doctoral studies candidate in agricultural economics at University College Dublin, Ireland. She holds a Master of Science from the UCD Michael Smurfit Graduate

Business School in Food Business Strategy and a Bachelor in Agricultural Science. Her research interests are the environmental, social and economic regional impacts of possible policy changes to the common agricultural policy. Anne has been a guest contributor to Mental Health for Millennials Volume 5 (2021) on the theme of resilience in Irish agriculture and Mental Health for Millennials Volume 6 (2022) on #hope for women in Irish agriculture. She has also been featured as a contributor in the TheDocCheck.Com published college studies series with her debut book.

Rachael Hussey is a journalism Master's Degree graduate who is predominantly a stay at home mother to her two small children and also works part time in the field of editing, content writing for social media and websites and has consulted for The Book Hub Publishing Group and contributed to the Dissertation Doctors Clinic. Rachael's Bachelor's degree is in English, Media and Cultural Studies from IADT and her Master's degree is from Dublin Institute of Technology.

Susan McKenna is Director of Book Hub Publishing where she is Commissioning Editor and Author Rep. She graduated in social care with a first class degree and has over two decades experience in social care practice and management. Susan is a former Erasmus Scholar (Stockholm) and Lectured p/t in Waterford and Athlone Institutes of Technology in addition to presenting workshops in east and west coast Canada. She has written widely on social care themes and is the co-author of two books in addition to having published several chapters in Book Hub Hub's Mental Health for Millennials Series (2017-2023).

Cathy Fitzgibbon is a sales and marketing professional in the media industry for the past three decades. She is passionate about exploring contemporary culinary experiences and actively promotes the areas of food sustainably and food tourism through her food writing contributions and marketing activities under her alias 'The Culinary Celt', using an ethically based farm to fork ethos. She has also contributed to several Book Hub Publishing books and TheDocCheck.Com publications in addition to presenting academic research papers both nationally and internationally. Cathy consults with The Dissertation Doctors clinic and most recently published her debut book, 'Eat With The Seasons'.

Jennifer Murphy MSc is a graduate of University of Limerick. Jennifer has worked for the past fourteen years in various Human Resources roles across several Retail, Manufacturing and Hospitality Sectors. A Highly strategic HR professional with a passion for Talent Management, Culture and Employment Legislation, she consults with TheDocCheck.Com in the area of HR and research perspectives and has contributed as a guest author in the recent series "Exploring Connectedness" and Mental Health for Millennials Vol 6. She is Director of The HR & Governance Suite.

Karen Gallen is a proud mum to two beautiful children, one of which has additional needs and is a 'scoliosis warrior'. Karen's focus is to shine light on additional needs and is an advocate for those with additional needs having recently been interviewed on national radio on the RTE Radio Drivetime programme on the theme of raising awareness on the range of 'other' difficulties facing parents of children with additional needs such as accommodation for hospital stays etc. She continues to be a support to other parents on online platforms by sharing her lived experience.

Karen's contributions on this matter can be read in Volume V in the Mental Health for Millennials book series and in the upcoming Volume VI of the same series, both published by The Book Hub Publishing Group.

Dr. Mary Helen Hensley is an internationally published author and a doctor of chiropractic. She was Book Hub Publishing's first published author back in 2009 and holds 'bestselling status.' Mary Helen is Head of Diversity, Inclusion and Equality at TheDocCheck.Com and regularly speaks and presents at international symposia and conferences where she is much sought after. She has published ten books and is a regular visitor to the

United States where she consults to the stars of Broadway and LA and is involved in a range of writing projects.

About TheDocCheck.Com

Based in Athenry, Galway and Limerick, Ireland, we provide full writing consulting solutions and academic coaching for your research needs. We help you develop the individual insights you will require to achieve your optimum grade or successful proposal, grant application or business plan completion.

We also specialise in content editing and document editing for the SME sector in addition to offering a suite of ghostwriting services.

Our multi-disciplinary team of nine consulting staff works with individuals and groups over the age of eighteen to fully enhance your research, writing and communications portfolios. We believe in excellence, in helping you to attain the best possible grade – and we have achieved this since 2007 with consistent honours grades awarded to our clients.

We work across all academic disciplines with qualitative and quantitative expertise, providing academic mentoring, one-to-one supervision for your research needs, thesis/project consulting solutions, proofreading, forensic editing and bespoke training.

Check out the many genuine reviews from real people Testimonials on our website, our Facebook Page, Instagram @DissertationDoctor or on our Twitter @ThesisClinic written by clients who have availed of, and believe in our service and have been kind enough to endorse us.

At this stage, we have worked with students and staff attending all of the Universities in Ireland and several in the UK and Canada, with Colleges in the former Institute of Technology sector and several private third-level colleges. We have sat on national education and assessment boards and have experience as external and internal examiners up to Doctoral level so know exactly what is sought to get you that magical grade! Even better, we cater for all academic disciplines.

Our specialists are excellent researchers and workshop presenters with the evaluative aptitude, critical knowledge, analytical proficiency and citation style expertise to get you through the process. We understand that Academic Departments differ in their thesis and dissertation criteria. That's why we make sure to accommodate the individual needs of each of our clients. We work with all of the major citation style formats.

Our Clinic staff are specialists in concepts that do not change; critical thinking, superior research design and development.

"THIS IS ONE HELL OF A TIME IN WHICH TO BE ALIVE."

ESSAYS ON COVID-19

We Decided Not Only To Try To Survive But To Thrive Amidst A Global Pandemic

Edited by Niall MacGiolla Bhui, PhD
Phil Noone, PhD

"We were inundated over the past two years as to how one might or might not become infected with Covid-19 and its subsequent variants. 'Science' changed weekly."

www.ingramcontent.com/pod-product-compliance
Lightning Source LLC
Chambersburg PA
CBHW051025030426
42336CB00015B/2730